DON'T DIE
in the WINTER
Your SEASON *Is* COMING

DR. MILLICENT HUNTER

Destiny Image® Publishers, Inc.
P.O. Box 310
Shippensburg, PA 17257-0310

*"Speaking to the Purposes of God for This Generation
and for the Generations to Come"*

ISBN 0-7684-2294-9
(Previously ISBN 1-56043-558-5)

For Worldwide Distribution

Printed in the U.S.A.

2 3 4 5 6 7 8 9 10/ 10 09 08 07 06 05

This book and all other Destiny Image, Revival Press, MercyPlace, Fresh Bread, Destiny Image Fiction, and Treasure House books are available at Christian bookstores and distributors worldwide.

To order books, call
1-800-722-6774.

For more information on foreign distributors, call
717-532-3040.

Or reach us on the Internet:
www.destinyimage.com

DEDICATION

This book is dedicated to my precious mother, Doris B. Hall, who is with the Lord. Because of you, Mother, the Deborah stood up in me. Also, to my dear father, Judge B. Hall, who is always there for me.

ACKNOWLEDGMENTS

ॐ

Thank you, Jason and Melissa, my precious children, for allowing me to fulfill God's will for my life. You are my greatest gifts from God. Always remember that you are strong, smart, and special. You are blessed and God is going to use you someday.

I deeply appreciate the sisterhood of the Governing Board of the E.C. Reems Women's International Ministries. You are powerful women of God: Bishop Barbara Amos, Pastor Claudette Copeland, Pastor Pamela Hines, Pastor Cynthia James, Evangelist Christine Liddell, Pastor Iona Locke, and Pastor Pat McKinstry. I admire your gifts and cherish your friendship. It is good to have a safe place. Remember Hawaii.

Words cannot express my gratitude for the wisdom and mentoring I have received from the most profound preachers of the 20th century, who have stimulated seeds of greatness in my life: Bishop Audrey Bronson, Pastor Ernestine Reems, and Pastor Rosie Wallace-Brown. I have benefited from your anointing as I sat under you and looked up to you.

To my father in the ministry, Dr. James S. Allen, Pastor of the Vine Memorial Baptist Church, who told me that the gospel must be preached.

To Dr. Janice Hodge, you have blessed my life. The God who creates really can restore. Reverend Carlita Henry and Pastor Saundra Hagans, God has blessed my life with your friendship. Evangelist Lisa Lee, you saw the magnitude of the vision even before I did. Thank you for obeying the Lord.

To my Executive Director of Millicent Hunter Ministries, Reverend Linda Pratt. Our meeting was divinely ordained of God. You have wisdom beyond your years and a level of expertise and professionalism that is unparalleled. Words cannot express my appreciation for the countless hours you spent helping me to transform my thoughts, words, scribbles, and ideas for this book, which will bless lives for years to come. You are destined to become one of the greatest preachers of the 21st century. You have understood that servanthood is a precursor to great leadership.

To my four distinguished siblings: Dr. Ron Hall, Attorney Judge Hall, Iva Hall-Fitch, and Barbara Hall-Harvin. You are precious to me.

To The Baptist Worship Center, the most loving and supportive congregation that any pastor could ever serve. I love you.

Finally, I give God praise for the Holy Spirit's guidance in the writing of this book.

CONTENTS

FOREWORD

⌁

In a day when many in the Body of Christ are experiencing tremendous attack and persecution from the enemy, believers must regain the urgency and compulsion to strive for intimacy with God. It is through this personal intimate walk with the Lord that we discover the true meaning of God's promise to never leave us or forsake us. In this day, very few books strike the reader as a permanent classic and an essential tool for the Christian life and ministry. This book, though, is one of them! *Don't Die in the Winter...* is one of the most important volumes for believers that I have read in a long time. It is filled with biblical understanding concerning most questions of the Christian life in terms of victory and deliverance from pain, hardship, and adversity. The Bible warns repeatedly that all Christians will struggle against satan and his spiritual forces of darkness. Although the spiritual conflict that you struggle against is very real, the answers are just as tangible. You can survive the winter! Don't wait any longer to discover that your most important defense against adversity is recognizing the enemy and knowing how to defeat him.

Dr. Millicent Hunter, Pastor of The Baptist Worship Center, is eminently qualified to give us helpful instruction on how to endure adversity by deepening our relationship with the Lord. She is a role model for many believers who are facing seemingly insurmountable odds in their walk with God. *Don't Die in the Winter...*speaks for itself. The mere creativity and uniqueness of the presentation of the various seasons of our life in Christ give us a fresh new look at this path we must all travel if we are to grow in Him. Millicent Hunter is unquestionably one of the most refreshing, radiant young preachers I know. She exemplifies in her personal life and ministry everything the apostle Paul meant when he spoke of the "fruit of the Spirit."

Dr. Hunter does not sugarcoat the Christian experience. She makes real to the reader the pain and hurt you face when you totally commit your life to God. But she does not stop there. The blessing of this book lies in the encouragement you will receive as you realize the power you possess to overcome. She gets right to the point and tells how to endure a winter season in your spiritual life. I am confident that no one can prayerfully read this book without becoming better equipped to handle the adversity that is sure to come. I believe that as you take your Bible and notebook and sit down to meditate upon the richness in this book, you will find that you have had a visitation from God.

Dr. Ernestine Cleveland Reems
Pastor, Center of Hope Community Church
Oakland, California

INTRODUCTION

This book is about endurance. It will bring clarity and understanding to all of the pain, problems, and persecution that you are going through. If you have cried out, "Why, God?" in the midst of adversity, this book will give you answers. You will also learn to defend yourself against satanic attack as you encounter the schemes of the evil one.

Living in the northeastern part of the country, I dread the coming of the winter months. In winter, everything is cold, drab, bleak, and still. But winter is the necessary hardship that we must pass through to get from fall to spring.

In the realm of spiritual things, a similar season lies between the fall of past expectations and the birth of new hopes and blessings. This is our "spiritual winter."

The terms of winter, wilderness, and valley experiences are used interchangeably to describe difficult places in our Christian experience. They are one and the same, and we all have to pass through them.

As you come to understand the reason for your winter season, your journey will have greater meaning. Not only will you learn to appreciate your sojourn there, but God also will strengthen your testimony with words that will glorify Him. I have not attempted to write an autobiography. Rather I have endeavored to describe, in clear detail, the seasonal changes of a believer's spiritual growth. To accomplish this task, though, I was forced again and again to refer to experiences in my own life. Just as I looked carefully at my own adversity to understand my winter season, you too must look carefully at your own life and hardship to understand your spiritual seasons. I have weathered the harshness of the most bitter winter seasons. *I know the way out, and I want to show that way to you.*

You will marvel at the faithfulness of God. This book will help you to prepare for winter. *Fortify yourself!* You will laugh, you will cry, you will question, and you will think. And if you "hold on" and "endure," when the season passes, you will "grow."

At the end of winter, you will see another season approaching. I call it your "due season." It is the season you have prayed for, waited for, and even cried for. Yes, your season of blessing is coming, but first, you must pass through the winter.

Because I have been in the depths of pain, darkness, and satanic attack, I have a deeper appreciation of the sunshine of God's blessings—and you will too.

I *had* to write this book for you!

Rev. Dr. Millicent Hunter
Pastor, The Baptist Worship Center

CHAPTER

1

OUR GOD IS A
SEASONAL GOD

ᔐ

Outside, the mercury climbed to 90 degrees in the warm sticky Philadelphia air. However, inside, the joyful sounds from the drums and organ drowned out the traffic and signaled the beginning of our service. Everything and everyone looked alive and vibrant.

The choir sang like an aggregation of angels. Every seat in the sanctuary occupied, the ushers looked helplessly for vacant seats in the balcony. Still more people filled the vestibule, waiting to enter. Six well-trained associate ministers graced the pulpit, and the congregation waited for me. Some sat wide-eyed and wondering. Others stood with their hands raised in worship. Still others praised the Lord in dance.

I looked out over the congregation and smiled. They looked like baby birds perched in a nest, beaks open wide enough to be fed. So, after praise and worship, I fed them. For nearly an hour I preached, taught, rebuked, reproved, whooped, and hollered. Even though I choked out many of my words, the Holy Spirit enabled me to minister life to the congregation.

Then, fighting back the tears, I stood in the pulpit and paused for a few moments. I was exhausted. Working from sunup to sundown to provide for my family, I had just joined the ranks of thousands of African-American women who are mothering and fathering a nation of black children.

Did the congregation hear the pain and brokenness in my voice? Weak and physically devastated from overwork, I leaned on my cane and extended the invitation to Christian discipleship. Fourteen souls came forward to accept Jesus Christ as Lord and Savior. The choir sang as if Heaven itself was coming down to greet them and the congregation erupted in a jubilation of praise.

Then time seemed to stand still for me. The Holy Spirit touched my heart in a place that no one could see. One thought after another rolled through my mind.

This was my second church and a pastor's dream. I had planted it 18 months ago. In 18 short months it had grown and thrived. I loved my church.

"It's beautiful, Lord, but why do I feel like running away?"

"I know, My daughter. I know. But, don't die in the winter; don't give up, spring is coming."

Winter? Yes, this was a spiritual winter, in spite of the summer heat that pressed down on the city. Fourteen new members only meant 14 new sets of problems, more tears to dry, more hurts to heal, and more souls to feed. Could I handle even one more spiritual baby? I felt like the old woman who lived in the shoe. I had so many children that I did not know what to do.

I had done all the right things. I was walking close to the Lord; I was well-educated and well-prepared. Positioned in a posture of total obedience and yieldedness before God, I expected blessings. Yet now, all hell was breaking loose in my life.

I mentally rehearsed some of the prophecies I had received, glowing words from individuals I greatly respected. *How did all of these ministry promises and my personal circumstances fit together?* Little did I know that my posture of obedience and yieldedness to the Lord had placed me in the "number one spot" on the devil's hit list.

I thought about the first church that I had been called to pastor. It was a mainline Baptist congregation and a unique setting because I was the first woman called to an African-American congregation in the city of Philadelphia.

I had pretended to struggle with the call on the outside because I knew about the animosity that many women pastors faced. But inside I knew, without a doubt, that God had called me.

My appointment to that church had stirred a tremendous amount of talk and attention, but the congregation embraced me and gave me a wonderful honeymoon experience. I also knew that this first church was just a proving ground for me. God had me there for a season of training and preparation.

Then the Lord planted a vision in my heart to start a new church and actually birth a work for Him. I saw a church reaching out to hurting people, bringing healing through the Word of God, and offering the ministry of love and reconciliation.

I knew God's calling on my life, but to my natural eye the situation and circumstances made it seem impossible. The timing appeared off. A single parent, rearing two young children barely out of diapers, I had a home to maintain and bills to pay.

I suggested to the Lord that perhaps He could wait until I raised my children and had some money and a building. Then I could follow His vision and obey His call. It made sense to me, but I had run away from God once before and found it futile. So I said "yes" to the Lord, and with this confession on my lips, planted The Baptist Worship Center and watched the congregation grow.

The church community watched me very closely. They wanted to see how this little woman was going to manage to raise two young children, work a secular job, keep food on her table, and pastor a new church at the same time—successfully.

I had a vision and a directive from God for this new ministry. Instead of the fruitful blessings I expected, however, the Spirit of God led me into the wilderness, into a spiritual season, where I met my enemy. I learned to survive the cold, the depth, the dry places, and the hopelessness of winter.

In spite of the harsh winter winds, I knew that my "season of fruitfulness" was coming. I could not afford to die in the winter and miss God. I had to learn how to protect myself against the deadly elements that attacked my ministry, my home, my family, and my physical body.

I could still hear the Holy Spirit speaking, *"Don't die in the winter; don't give up; spring is coming."* No, I would not die!

My drifting thoughts returned to the church service and the new converts gathered at the altar. The choir director must have noticed the exhaustion in my weak body. He signaled a coming song and I nodded in approval. All over the congregation, the sweet sounds of "Amazing Grace" filled the air and I stepped forward to welcome 14 new souls into the Kingdom of God.

FROM GLORY TO GLORY

All over the Body of Christ, Christians are learning to understand, prepare for, and endure their spiritual winters. Our lives are in a process of continual change. Although God is the same yesterday, today, and forever, He is continually transforming us. Paul tells us that "we...are changed into the same image from glory to glory, even as by the Spirit of the Lord" (2 Cor. 3:18).

Every living thing passes through seasons of change. Some seasons are easy, even pleasant, to pass through. Others are very difficult. Our God is a seasonal God. Solomon said:

To every thing there is a season, and a time to every purpose under the heaven: a time to be born, and a time to die; a time to plant, and a time to pluck up that which is planted; a time to kill, and a time to heal; a time to break down, and a time to build up; a time to weep, and a time to laugh; a time to mourn, and a time to dance; a time to cast away stones, and a time to gather stones together; a time to embrace, and a time to refrain from embracing; a time to get, and a time to lose; a time to keep, and a time to cast away; a time to rend, and a time to sew; a time to keep silence, and a time to speak; a time to love, and a time to hate; a time of war, and a time of peace (Ecclesiastes 3:1-8).

There is a right time for everything, and everything has its season. The secret to peace in God is to discover, expect, and appreciate God's perfect timing in your life.

God Shows Us Through Creation

God has so designed our earth that there are four natural divisions of the year: spring, summer, fall, and winter. Each natural division begins as the sun passes through the corresponding solstice known as the equinox. Every geographical location experiences these natural seasonal divisions to one degree or another.

And God said, Let there be lights in the firmament of the heaven to divide the day from the night; and let them be for signs, and for seasons, and for days, and years (Genesis 1:14).

Each division of the year is called a season, and it is characterized by certain changes. There is the rainy season, the dry

19

season, the planting season, the harvest season, the hunting season, and the hurricane season. Our God is a seasonal God! "Nevertheless He…gave us rain from heaven, and fruitful seasons, filling our hearts with food and gladness" (Acts 14:17).

Spring arrives and the earth is made ready for planting. We till the fallow ground, watch the grass grow, enjoy the flowers that bloom, and listen to the birds sing.

The hot season of summer follows spring. Activities increase. Life is in full bloom and this is the time of nurturing and fertilization. Excitement builds in the summer. Everybody wants to be in love. People are going here and there. Our lives are filled with activities.

Then fall comes and brings a chill to the air. Activities slow down and our focus changes. The days grow shorter and the nights get longer. Folks begin to gather in and settle down for the coming months.

Winter arrives and the birds fly south. The sun hugs the earth and wears a frosty overcoat. Animals hibernate and all of nature cooperates when winter comes.

LIFE CHANGES TEACH US

Not only are there seasons in the natural realm, but we have seasons in our physical lives as well. From the moment we are conceived in our mother's womb, a human growth cycle is set in motion, one that brings about certain biological changes. This growth cycle is separated into specific divisions much like seasons.

This cycle is governed and characterized by the development and the maturity of the various body systems. The cells multiply and they become a zygote. This completes a season. The zygote then becomes an embryo and that is a season.

The embryo becomes a fetus. There are bumps for the eyes and buds for the ears. Arms and legs begin to appear, and fingers and toes become differentiated. Every division of growth is characterized by certain changes until the fetus reaches a certain level of maturity and is ready to be birthed forth.

Thou hast covered me in my mother's womb. I will praise Thee; for I am fearfully and wonderfully made... (Psalm 139:13b-14).

Our growth cycle does not stop with the initial stages of fetal development, however. Every millisecond of our existence, from birth to childhood, adulthood to death, we are constantly changing.

We are different in some way today from what we were yesterday. There will be something different about each individual tomorrow that is not evident today. Some of these changes are so very subtle that they go completely unnoticed and undetected, but they are there.

One hundred hairs fell out of our head yesterday. One thousand skin cells fell off of our upper epidermal layer this morning. Most of us have a little more knowledge in our head today than we had yesterday. Our physical body is 24 hours older today than it was yesterday. Every moment of our lives we are changing.

Sometimes change is upsetting and disquieting because it disturbs the boundaries of our comfort zone. In our comfort zone we know what is coming next. There is no need to be on guard or to watch our backs. We just "go with the flow." Life is comfortable.

I remember when my hair turned gray prematurely. I was 30 years old, single, and upset! This disturbed my comfort zone. I did what I knew how to do. I fasted, prayed, anointed my head with oil, and bought a bottle of Clairol to chase the gray away. But as life is, change is inevitable and completely unavoidable.

PASSING THROUGH SPIRITUAL SEASONS

We experience the full depth of all four seasons in our spiritual growth. So if we are to mature in the things of God, we need to adapt to seasonal changes.

Those of us who are spiritually sensitive are keenly aware of a tremendous moving and shaking taking place in the Body of Christ. A great deal of the status quo is changing. Traditions and customs are changing. Old habits, practices, rules, and regulations are coming under close scrutiny, and change is evident.

Remember ye not the former things, neither consider the things of old. Behold, I will do a new thing; now it shall spring forth; shall ye not know it? I will even make a way in the wilderness, and rivers in the desert (Isaiah 43:18-19).

God prepares His people to do battle with the enemy. This preparation molds us, makes us, designs us, and shapes us. In the process we are pruned, tested, and tried in order to conform to the image of His Son. "For whom He did foreknow, He also did predestinate to be conformed to the image of His Son..." (Rom. 8:29).

Many Christians are going through situations that are very difficult to understand. But just as there are seasons and specific times of growth and development in the human body, so there are seasons, or specific times of growth and development, in our spiritual lives.

JESUS IS OUR BIBLICAL EXAMPLE

Jesus was baptized in the Jordan River by John and *led by the Spirit* into the wastelands of Judea, where satan tempted Him 40 days. *The Holy Spirit led Him into the wilderness.* (See Luke 4:1-2.)

A wilderness is a desolate place. Everything is dry, arid, and parched. The wilderness does not have a comfort zone. It has no solace, rest, relief, or reprieve. But Jesus was *led* "by the Spirit into the wilderness."

Most of us want to believe that if the Holy Spirit is leading us, He will always lead us beside still waters. But, just like Jesus, sometimes the Holy Spirit leads us into dry and desolate places where there is no rest, relief, or comfort. It is a spiritual season that we must pass through, just as Jesus did. Circumstances do not tell us whether we are *in* or *out* of God's will; relationship alone does that.

God sent Ezekiel to a valley of dry bones. The place Ezekiel had to go was unpleasant, but the Spirit of God *led* him there (see Ezek. 37:1).

The Spirit also led the apostle Paul into his "wilderness" experiences.

Thrice was I beaten with rods, once was I stoned, thrice I suffered shipwreck, a night and a day I have been in the deep; in journeyings often, in perils of waters, in perils of robbers, in perils by mine own countrymen, in perils by the heathen, in perils in the city, in perils in the wilderness, in perils in the sea, in perils among false brethren; in weariness and painfulness, in watchings often, in hunger and thirst, in fastings often, in cold and nakedness (2 Corinthians 11:25-27).

WHAT IS A WINTER SEASON?

What is it like to be in the wilderness in winter? In the natural we know there are four seasons, and if you live in an area that experiences the full depth of all four seasons, when it is winter, you know it is winter. Spring, summer, and fall are also clearly differentiated. If you are from Chicago, the windy

23

city, or Florida, the sunshine state, seasonal changes are not as clearly defined.

But in certain areas like Philadelphia, for the most part, when it is winter, there is no doubt about it. You know it is winter. When it is summer, the pollen count, the humidity, and the sweat on your brow let you know that it is summer. Here we experience the full depth of all four seasons and we learn to adapt to those seasonal changes.

The winter season is a cold, drab time of year. Everything is bleak in the winter. Negative things happen in the winter. Cold sets in and contrary winds blow. The birds fly south and the bears go into hibernation. The leaves turn brown and fall to the ground. The plants die, water freezes up, and fish travel downstream. The sky gets gray, days get shorter, and accident rates go up. The crime rate goes up. Bills get higher. People get more depressed in winter because they cannot be as productive as they are in the summer.

Sometimes people are not as excited about the things of God in the winter. In the church house there is a great "falling away" of the children of God. People do not want to press their way through the winter snow and the harsh cold weather to come to the house of God. The devil uses this as an opportunity to kill the spirit of faith.

The apostle Paul even pointed to his ministry in the churches as part of his trials. "Besides those things that are without, that which cometh upon me daily, the care of all the churches" (2 Cor. 11:28).

The Bible would have us to know that there are certain seasons in the life of every believer. Our God is a seasonal God. A winter season in your life, spiritually speaking, is a season when everything that can go wrong will go wrong. The foundation will be shaken. You may feel like the walls are closing in, and every time you turn around there might be trouble. Jesus warned us that there would be winter seasons in this life. "In the world ye shall have tribulation..." (Jn. 16:33b).

A winter season is to have a son or a daughter strung out on drugs and not be able to do anything about it. A winter season is to get an eviction notice and not know where the rent money is coming from. A winter season is getting a pink slip from your job or a frightening diagnosis from your doctor. That is a winter season.

The devil comes at us when everything is cold, dark, and bleak. He comes when we reach a spiritual low. We become relaxed in our prayer life, our time with God, our Bible study, and fellowship with the saints in the house of God.

The enemy often chooses his time of attack when we are not built up in the inner man. Many of us are dying in our seats. We go to the house of God and we are hurting inside. A slow spiritual death is overtaking us and we are trying to cover it up. Songs that we used to sing no longer excite us. Clapping fails to reach our hands and we no longer have dancing in our feet. We are ready for the devil's attack. Of course, he cannot read our mind, but he can watch our behavior and choose his time of attack.

> *Be sober, be vigilant; because your adversary the devil, as a roaring lion, walketh about, seeking whom he may devour* (1 Peter 5:8).

The devil will not only attack you, but he will attack your household by coming into your camp and your sanctuary. If he can, he will touch everybody in your house at the same time.

Many Christians are in a winter season right now. The devil has set up camp in their house. Many are sleeping with the enemy, eating with the enemy, and waking up with the enemy. The enemy is in their house, talking to them, telling them what to do and what not to do.

They do not understand why all of this is taking place and they do not understand why God has not delivered them yet.

WHY ARE SPIRITUAL WINTERS NECESSARY?

When the Spirit of God leads us into the wilderness, we may find ourselves in difficult places. We are not always there because of sin in our life, or because of unwise choices. Sometimes we find ourselves in the wilderness simply because the Spirit of God has *led* us there.

The Spirit *led* Jesus into the wilderness for a time of testing, trying, and tempting. Why was it necessary for Jesus to be tempted to sin?

First, temptation is part of the human experience. Because Jesus was fully God and fully human, He had to understand what we endure in this life. He had to experience what we experience.

Second, Jesus had to undo Adam's work. Adam, though perfect, gave into temptation and consequently passed on sin to the entire human race. Jesus, by contrast, resisted satan and teaches us, by example, how to endure trials and testing, and how to resist the temptation to sin.

And Jesus answered him, saying, It is written, That man shall not live by bread alone, but by every word of God. ... And Jesus answered and said unto him, Get thee behind Me, satan: for it is written, Thou shalt worship the Lord thy God, and Him only shalt thou serve. ... And Jesus answering said unto him, It is said, Thou shalt not tempt the Lord thy God (Luke 4:4,8,12).

If we tell Jesus, "Nobody knows the trouble I've seen," Jesus says, "I do; I've been there."

Temptation at High Points

Temptation often comes after a high point in our spiritual lives. When we are at a high point, it is a good season. We look good, sound good, and feel good. Everything we touch turns to gold.

Satan chooses the time for his attacks. He likes to tempt us through our strengths, especially when we are susceptible to pride and a haughty spirit. Paul warned Timothy against this: "…lest being lifted up with pride he fall into the condemnation of the devil" (1 Tim. 3:6).

Jesus was about to come into His best season. He had spent 29 years of His life learning, maturing, and preparing in life and in the things of God. He had just been baptized by John. The voice of His Father had spoken from Heaven, saying, "Thou art My beloved Son; in Thee I am well pleased" (Lk. 3:22b). The Holy Spirit, in the form of a dove, had settled upon His shoulders.

He was about to birth forth into His own ministry and fulfill the purpose for which He came. He needed to preach, teach, heal, and deliver. He would die for the sins of the world, be resurrected, and seal our redemption forever. Yet He still had to suffer and pass through this wilderness, this winter season.

Being forty days tempted of the devil. And in those days He did eat nothing: and when they were ended, He afterward hungered (Luke 4:2).

The devil worked on Jesus for 40 days and 40 nights. Many of us have difficulty going through something for 40 minutes. But Jesus was tempted for 40 days. He fasted and prayed. He was weak physically because He ate nothing and drank nothing, but He was strong spiritually. The human part of Him was at an all-time low, but the divine part of Him was at an all-time high.

Do Not Abort the Will of God

Many Christians are about to birth forth a ministry. God has impregnated the Body of Christ with many gifts and abilities and the Church is in travail. Christians are going through some difficult things because the season of labor is painful and hard.

Perhaps you have been impregnated with a vision for ministry, a mighty work to do for the Lord, but you have not quite given birth to it yet. It has not fully come forth yet.

The Lord is saying, "Before there can be a child in this natural realm, there must be a season of labor."

But some of us want to get off the table, take our feet out of the stirrups, turn the monitors off, and abort the entire process. We want to abort the will of God in our lives because the labor is too hard, because we are going through difficult changes, because we are in a difficult season in our lives, because the test is too hard, and because the travailing is too hard. Some will simply give up and die because the winter is too long and too cold.

This is the time and the decade when the saints must bruise the serpent's head. We must determine to live, to see this birth through, and to press into the next season fully prepared, so God can use us!

Brethren...this one thing I do, forgetting those things which are behind, and reaching forth unto those things which are before, I press toward the mark for the prize of the high calling of God in Christ Jesus (Philippians 3:13-14).

Zion is about to unveil the full manifestation of the sons and daughters of God. From city to city, from state to state, from one local body of Christ to another, people are giving birth in the Spirit. This is our manifested hour. This is the time when we shall rise up, go forth, and do what God has called us to do. We shall rise up above the devil and take back what is rightfully ours. God has promised this in His Word.

And I will restore to you the years that the locust hath eaten.... And ye shall eat in plenty, and be satisfied, and praise the name of the Lord your God... (Joel 2:25-26).

Temptation at Low Points

The devil also tempts us during the times that we are the most vulnerable, when we are tired, lonely, and weighing big decisions in our lives. The devil taps into our weak spot. He comes during our lowest of lows, when we cannot see our way, when we are frustrated and devastated, when everybody gets on our nerve and our reserve nerve. This is when the enemy comes in and tempts for a season, as warned in First Peter: "...though now for a season, if need be, ye are in heaviness through manifold temptations" (1 Pet. 1:6).

Jesus was at a low point physically. His body was weak and the human side of Him was at an all-time low. Jesus was not tempted in the temple. He was not tempted at His baptism. He was tempted in the wilderness where He was tired, alone, hungry, and vulnerable.

The Devil Knows

Satan knows when God is getting ready to do something in your life. The enemy knew that Jesus was about to birth forth into the fullness of His ministry to accomplish that great act of salvation and redemption.

The devil knows when God is getting ready to bless you, to use you, to move in you, to promote you, and to fully bring you forth. When the hand of God is upon your life, the devil is drawn to you.

Demons are attracted to your anointing. The devil does not bother you when you are casual and lukewarm about the things of God because you are not a threat to his kingdom. Oh, but if you keep trying to live holy and continue walking on the path of righteousness for His name's sake, you will find yourself in the wilderness in a bitter winter season—tired, alone, spiritually hungry, and vulnerable.

DO NOT DIE IN THE WINTER

I believe Paul had an urgency in his spirit to tell the people, "Whatever you do, don't die in the winter. You have got to learn how to endure hardship as a good soldier. It doesn't matter how hard things get, you must understand that it's only for a season."

Winter does not stay all year long. Spring is just around the corner. We have got to learn how to hang in there because it is only for a season. You must understand that trials will come your way.

We must learn how to adapt to seasonal changes. We have to prepare for and protect ourselves from spiritual winters just as we do from the dangers of natural winters. The perils and pitfalls of seasonal changes must be resisted.

The devil knows us and he knows all about us. He knows whether or not we have established a pattern of resistance. Just as a weak body catches a cold easily, we can catch all kinds of illnesses that are spiritually-oriented when our spiritual resistance is low.

Some of us are overtaken by every little thing in our life and we are susceptible to everything that the enemy does. Some of us have been suffering through some difficult things in our lives for a very long time—in fact, it has been so long that we think suffering is a way of life. We think that we are supposed to suffer. We think that we are supposed to hurt all the time. But God says, *"I gave unto you power and it's up to you to tell the devil 'I take authority over you' when you want him to leave you alone."*

The battleground, you see, is in your mind.

For we wrestle not against flesh and blood, but against principalities, against powers, against the rulers of the darkness of this world, against spiritual wickedness in high places (Ephesians 6:12).

For though we walk in the flesh, we do not war after the flesh: (for the weapons of our warfare are not carnal, but mighty through God to the pulling down of strong holds;) casting down imaginations, and every high thing that exalteth itself against the knowledge of God, and bringing into captivity every thought to the obedience of Christ (2 Corinthians 10:3-5).

ESTABLISH A PATTERN OF RESISTANCE

If the enemy can control your mind, he can control your behavior. Get ready to resist him. Prepare yourself for the winter.

1. Put on the full armor of God (Eph. 6:13-17).

2. Protect yourself with the Word of God (Eph. 6:17b; 2 Tim. 3:16-17; Heb. 4:12).

3. Prepare yourself with prayer (Eph. 6:18; Phil. 4:6).

4. Learn how to praise Him at all times (Phil. 4:4; Eph. 5:19-20).

5. Submit yourself to God, resist satan, and he will run from you (Jas. 4:7).

SPRING WILL COME

After you have come through great turmoil and great suffering, you will see a ray of sunshine and begin to feel the refreshing power of God.

31

Spring will set in and cloudy days will be pushed back. The cold weather will subside and the leaves will begin to grow again. The rain will cease. The flowers will begin to bloom and the harsh cold bitterness of winter will abate. The grass that you thought was dead will begin to grow again in spring. Whatever you do in your spiritual life, *"don't die in the winter."* Your best season is coming.

When your season comes, everything changes. A metamorphosis takes place in your spirit. Every child of God must go through changes in order to develop and grow. You cannot afford to remain the same.

Look at the caterpillar. He appears to die in the winter because he is hard, cold, and still. But when spring comes the caterpillar sprouts wings and flies as a butterfly. So God says to those who are dying in the Spirit:

> *"You've got to go through a spiritual metamorphosis in order to take flight and soar to the spiritual heights that I have assigned to your life. You cannot afford to die because your season is on its way.*

> *"You may appear to be dead now. You may appear to be lost. You may appear to be down now, but if you hold on and hold out, if you stay close to Me, there is a deliverance.*

> *You'll soon hear birds chirping and bees buzzing. You'll feel the sun beaming down on your head. You must refuse to die. You must believe that I have a season of blessing for you."*

When I look around the Church, I see others passing through the winter season. Some are dying in the midst of it. It is frustrating to watch this happen because the Church should be a place of life, not death.

I see signs of death when the ushers lose their joy and put on sour faces. I hear signs of death in lifeless singing. I can also hear it in the noneffective, dry, lifeless sermons of the preacher who stares down at his manuscript and merely regurgitates dead words. He goes through the motions of preaching without life, joy, or power.

The people in the pew become so accustomed to death that they are satisfied with it. The house of God is a place of life, not death!

I have cried out to God many times, "Lord, I want to reach the high places in You. I don't want to sit in the church and die spiritually. I want to go higher in You."

We almost expect God to mystically pour something into us, give us a personal relationship pill, or deposit in us more grace.

However, the Lord reminded me, "*I am not neglecting you. I heard you when you prayed the first time. I have the prescription, but I am taking you through places in My own way to give you what you are praying for.*"

I have come to understand that this is not something we ask for and receive instantaneously. We ask to reach a certain place in God and then God takes us *through something to get to that place.*

I refuse to die because I know that the blessing is coming. I have seen the seasonal cycle take place in my own life and ministry. I know that springtime always follows winter.

GOD IS A GOD OF TIMELY BLESSINGS

God is watching you. He is waiting to see what you are going to do. God has to know that He can trust you. Some of you are losing your conviction and compromising your faith. You are sitting down, giving up, and dying in the winter.

God chooses our time of blessing. He knows just when to bless us, where to bless us, and how to bless us. Perhaps you have been praying about something for days, weeks, months, or years, but God has not brought it to pass yet. You feel like you are in the valley of the shadow of death; you feel as if you are having a wilderness experience.

You wonder, *How did I ever get here and what did I ever do to deserve this?*

The Spirit of God has *led* you to a time of testing and trials so when He does bless you and bring you forth, you will be anointed with all power and authority on earth. *"Don't die in the winter!"*

The Spirit of the Lord is saying, *"Get up, square your shoulders, clear your head, and praise Me! Walk like you have the victory because your season of blessing is coming."*

CHAPTER

2

THE FOUR SEASONS
IN YOUR LIFE

⳽

SPRING

God has always used the pictures of nature to tell us about Himself, His character, and even ourselves. Creation itself reveals what God is like. All we have to do is to look very closely at the things He has put in front of us.

Paul tells us that ever since the creation of the world, God's eternal power and divine nature, invisible though they are, have been understood and seen through the things He has made.

> *For the invisible things of Him from the creation of the world are clearly seen, being understood by the things that are made, even His eternal power and Godhead...* (Romans 1:20).

What kind of God does nature reveal? Nature shows us a God of might, intelligence, and intricate detail; a God of order and beauty; a God who controls powerful forces.

GOD'S PEOPLE ARE LIKE TREES

God's Word presents a creative analogy between people and trees. We can find many parallels for our own Christian experience.

But I am like a green olive tree in the house of God: I trust in the mercy of God for ever and ever (Psalm 52:8).

The righteous shall flourish like the palm tree: he shall grow like a cedar in Lebanon (Psalm 92:12).

And he shall be like a tree planted by the rivers of water... (Psalm 1:3).

If a tree is planted as a seed in the springtime, all of the conditions for the seed, and the little seedling to come, should be perfect. It needs to be planted in good soil, enriched with fertilizer, and watered faithfully. If these conditions are present, the seed will germinate and grow according to the Creator's plan.

And God said, Let the earth bring forth grass, the herb yielding seed, and the fruit tree yielding fruit after his kind, whose seed is in itself, upon the earth: and it was so (Genesis 1:11).

WE BEGIN FROM A HOLY SEED

When we accept the Lord Jesus Christ as personal Savior, God plants the seed of the Holy Spirit within us. Hopefully, our lives are good soil for this seed. I accepted Christ at the tender age of nine and this seed was planted in my life.

Something else usually happens during the first springtime of our spiritual lives. When we plant a seed prayer, then if this prayer is watered and cultivated—it ultimately develops into our life focus for God, or our "calling." We might begin to ask the Lord to "use us for His glory," or to "give us a burden for souls." If He has touched our life in a unique way, such as in physical healing, we might ask Him to use us to bring healing to others. These prayers are seeds that need to mature with the passing seasons of our lives.

God revealed to me, at the age of 9, His call upon my life. Even then I knew that I would be a preacher and a pastor. This was a crazy notion for a young child like me because I had no role models to suggest that this could be a reality for my life.

For many years I enjoyed church and thrived as a young seedling. Church was a fun place and the center of all social activity in my life. I was sheltered from the world and nurtured in the church. It was just like being in a hothouse, having all my needs met. As the seedling of faith in my life was fertilized, watered, and cared for, it took root and began to grow.

SUMMER

The light and warmth of the summer sun helps the seedling to continue to grow to a sapling. Summers are filled with activity. People feel very much alive. The birds sing and the rain is sweet. I have had these times in my life; just me and Jesus, Jesus and me. I had no bills, no problems, and no major decisions to make. Everyone was happy and the warmth of the sun was focused on me.

In summer, the weather is usually very pleasant and often predictable. But a sapling has to learn to withstand threatening summer storms and scorching heat. Summer is the time that young plants are moved from the protective, controlled environment of the seedbed to a larger pot to encourage growth. Here the surroundings are less predictable. The young plant has to adjust to its new environment.

I was replanted in my teen years when I left for college. I had to learn to withstand the controversy of the people around me who questioned the authenticity of God. The doubts of the world, which came at me like summer windstorms, had to be withstood. I also had to learn how to deal with the scornful looks from the intellectual community when the subject of salvation arose. However, my personal needs were still met and my first summer "season" as a Christian was a good one.

FALL

In the fall the tree is removed from the artificial environment of the hothouse to a garden or field. The opportunity for growth increases, but the conditions are different. The safety of the flower pot and the constant attention of the nursery caretaker are gone.

The little sapling has to adjust to weather conditions and learn how to thrive on its own, relying on its root system to search for and absorb minerals from the soil. The roots begin to sink deep into the earth to anchor the sapling. It continues to grow and learns how to endure changing weather conditions, parasites, and the threat of annihilation by wild animals.

Outside the safety of my church, I was not always surrounded by believers. It seemed as if the unbelievers, in the world, were having a better time than I was. I never walked away from the church, but I did keep a foot in both places for a time. The Lord, in His mercy, kept a hedge of protection around me, just like a concerned farmer might fence in his young trees to keep the wild animals out. I had to learn to thrive on my own, relying on my roots that ran deep in Jesus to anchor me.

A good farmer will notice if one sapling is leaning a little bit to the left or to the right. I have seen young trees with wire and rubber tubing around them to keep them straight. Similarly, even though I bent a little bit this way or a little bit that way, I always had that protective tubing and wire around me so I would not bend over and break. I did lean to the side a little, but I continued to grow in God.

FALL PRUNING

Pruning takes place in the fall. Orchard growers prune or cut back the branches to remove the superfluous branches. This improves the shape of the tree, encourages growth, increases fruitfulness, and makes the fruit easier to reach. Each season of pruning produces growth.

Jesus makes a distinction between two kinds of pruning: (a) separating and (b) cutting back the branches. Fruit trees are cut back to promote the proper kind of growth. In other words, sometimes God must discipline us to strengthen our character and faith.

Branches that do not bear fruit are cut off at the trunk. Not only are they worthless, but they often infect the rest of the tree. Those who do not bear fruit for God, or who try to block the efforts of God's people, will be cut off from the divine flow of life.

Every branch in Me that beareth not fruit He taketh away: and every branch that beareth fruit, He purgeth it, that it may bring forth more fruit (John 15:2).

The maturity of a tree can be determined by counting the rings in the trunk. These rings are markings that say, "This tree went through a period of successful growth. It endured the adversity of weather and environmental conditions and survived." Ten rings signifies ten seasons of successful growth.

When we survive pain and adversity in our life, we are left with markings that say, "I was wounded, I endured, and I survived. Here are the rings to prove it." These markings are the Christlike characteristics that are developed in us as a result of surviving hardship. They are reminders that say, "I've been through a season of adversity and I have survived."

If we look at a piece of fine furniture that has been fashioned from the wood of a tree, the more markings and rings that we see, the greater the beauty of the wood. Even though man sometimes attempts to reproduce these markings in wood veneer, the real beauty of natural wood can never be captured and reproduced in a facade.

The beauty of our relationship with God lies in our growth and willingness to submit to the pruning knife. We can speak the right words, but our testimony does not become authentic until we have withstood the trials that prune us. Spiritual pruning cuts away the superficiality in our life.

Many things hinder our spiritual growth, even though we are not aware of it. For example, we think that we have love and compassion for other people, but until the Lord brings a person into our midst who is unlovable, our true level of love is minimal and untested.

JESUS IS THE VINE

Jesus tells us that He is the Vine and the Father is the Vinegrower who cares for the branches to make them fruitful (see Jn. 15:1-8). The branches all claim to be followers of Christ. However, the fruitful branches are true believers who, by their living union with Christ, produce much fruit. But the unproductive branches (those who turn from following Christ after making a superficial commitment) will be separated from the Vine. Unproductive followers are as good as dead. They will be cut off and cast aside.

When a vine bears "much fruit," God is glorified because He has sent the sunshine and rain to make the crop grow. He has constantly nurtured the tiny plant and prepared it to blossom. When the fruit harvest comes, the Lord of the harvest is glorified. This farming analogy shows us that God is glorified when people come into a right relationship with Him and begin to "bear much fruit" in their lives.

During the pruning process a tree often bleeds sap. The caretaker binds up the open branches so the tree will remain strong. The sap itself solidifies and acts like a bandage over the open cut.

There is a season, however, in the life of certain maple trees, when men actually collect the sap from trees. When the sap comes forth in the proper season, it is wonderful. It makes our pancakes and waffles come alive, but when "out of season," it is bitter and tasteless.

God desires to manifest wonderful works as He develops talents and abilities within us. However, these gifts are not always sweet and palatable until they stay in their place and are sweetened by adversity and the enduring power of the Holy Spirit. This must all take place in the "proper season."

In the Christian life, branches can be characteristic of our spiritual development in specific areas. One branch represents our love for others. One is forgiveness, one is mercy, and another is generosity. Each one of these branches must be pruned by God. Just as a caretaker prunes a tree, God allows us to be cut by circumstances in particular areas of our life. This is necessary for greater growth in those areas and, thereby, for greater potential for ministry.

THE LORD PRUNED MY LIFE

I found security in a lot of people and things (a good education, a wonderful home life, and a very stable, large traditional church). Everything was comfortable for me.

As the Lord began to prune me, He showed me that my education in God is an ongoing, lifelong process. God showed me my dependence on loving supportive people. They were pruned out of my life. I fought against this in prayer, but the Lord allowed it to take place. My security blanket disappeared.

He showed me my future ministry. I saw people damaged by broken relationships, pain, and despair; people stuck in a valley of hopelessness. It was not going to be enough to pat them on the head and say, "God will make a way somehow." I had to journey to the valley of hopelessness myself, set up camp there, and learn to survive.

I have never met a person who has not struggled with or suffered deep wounds as a result of a broken relationship. Whether this brokenness occurs in a dysfunctional family, from abuse, with the loss of a loved one, or in a failed relationship, all human pain has its genesis in human relationship. This is why a deep, sincere, abiding, and intimate relationship with God is so vital to our lives. God has created us to have relationship with Him.

Hopelessness is a dark valley, but crisis drives us deeper into the bosom of God. I lived in the valley and I not only survived the wilderness, but I learned to flourish over a period of time. The wilderness became less threatening, less harsh; it became *even pleasant* because I learned to search for beauty and meaning in the emptiness and adversity. The beauty is found in the intimacy one develops with God.

You cannot lead someone else on a path that you yourself have not traveled. The Lord told me that I would return to that valley, that wilderness, that cold place of winter, many times to search for hurting people.

I knew the way in and I knew the way out. Just as Harriet Tubman returned to the slave-holding South many times, amidst threats of death, to rescue her people, I too would return in search of God's hurting people. I would bring healing, hope, a word of encouragement, and a plan showing them the way out.

The branches in my life experienced a tremendous severing and cutting, but those are the ones that have flourished and reproduced to the greatest extent.

PRUNING ALWAYS HAS PURPOSE

The bonsai tree is an art form. Its beauty is revealed, not in height or stature, but in how it reaches out as it is cut back. As we are pruned, our branches reach out. We are not meant to grow spiritually big and tall so that we are beautiful to the eye of man, however. The beauty in the bonsai is that it is small—although it is not insignificant. Our beauty is in our humility before God and in our Christlike spirit that reaches out to other people.

Fruit trees are pruned to remain small. The fruit must be within reach to be picked. Many individuals in ministry are only interested in growing tall, but the people who need their spiritual fruit cannot reach it. God is careful not to let us grow so far above the people we minister to that they cannot reach the fruit in our lives.

A GREAT FALLING AWAY

Not only did the weather change in the fall, but I found "a great falling away" of people around me. During my college years I experienced an interest in different philosophies and religions. They piqued my curiosity, but my roots in the church were so deep and so strong that I did not fall away. However, I was not satisfied with mediocrity. I desired a deeper relationship with the Lord.

I met believers who seemed to have something I did not have and I knew that I was missing something. I said to the Lord, "I don't know what it is that they have, but whatever it is, I want it."

Although I did not have the spiritual ears to hear it at the time, I believe God was whispering, "*These believers have learned to pass through the seasons of life. They know how to endure the winter and move full circle back into the springtime of their spiritual lives. And you too, My daughter, will learn to stand against the*

45

harsh realities of the winter winds in order to be of greater service to Me. For without the winter, there can be no spring."

WINTER

Winter is inevitable in the life of every believer, and the first bitter experience is often the most difficult one to pass through. We are not certain what to expect or what to do. In the natural, we learn to be prepared because of previous experience. We know that the temperature drops so we prepare our homes, clothing, and food.

The scheme of creation prepares the tree by dropping its leaves and pulling all of its life resources deep into the branches, trunk, and roots. Winter is not a time of growth for the tree; it is a time of endurance and testing. If the roots have sunk deeply enough, if its overall health is good, and if the young tree is given adequate protection by the farmer, it will survive the chilly winds of winter and the cold blanket of snow.

It began to snow in my life. The weather turned cold, the sky gray, and the outlook bleak. After reading the book, *Hinds' Feet on High Places*, I started to pray lofty prayers. I told God, "Lord, I want hinds' feet on high places! I want more of You!"

The Lord God is my strength, and He will make my feet like hinds' feet, and He will make me to walk upon mine high places... (Habakkuk 3:19).

The Lord showed me that there are many who desire to walk forward in Christ, but there are few who are willing to climb as well. Climbing requires effort. You have to hoist yourself up and exert energy in order to climb.

A person recovering from a medical condition is often encouraged to walk, but not to climb stairs. Going down stairs just requires keeping steady, but climbing up takes all of one's energy. Our walk with the Lord in winter is like that. We have to hoist ourselves up and exert spiritual energy.

The Lord told me, *"If you want to rise up to the higher places in Me, it will involve climbing; and climbing always involves struggle. Is this really what you want?"*

Once I said "yes" and began climbing, the first steps were quite easy because I was energetic and strong. The first ones are always easy, but the higher we have to climb, the more difficult it becomes.

THE ENEMY COMES IN THE WINTER

Winter arrived and the enemy attacked me in every way possible. First, he targeted my physical body with the deadly disease called meningitis. Within 24 hours I found myself delirious with pain, lying in the emergency room, my life hanging in the balance between life and death. I was not expected to live. *That was a wilderness.*

Meningitis is an inflammation of the fluids surrounding the brain. It starts out with a simple headache and is often misdiagnosed as tension or stress.

I exhausted every Scripture I knew, but it was hard to find faith in the valley. They moved me to a room in Intensive Care, where I would remain for two weeks. I lay motionless in a hospital bed with IV's piercing the flesh of both arms and a monitor keeping track of my weakening heart. Cleaning my bathroom or taking out the trash would have been a welcome change from the loneliness and isolation I felt in that room.

I know how it feels to be gravely ill. It is lonely. The mind has plenty of time to think. Illness is like a dark, haunting valley. Sickness is cold and gray like winter. I cried out to the Lord, "I am here all by myself!"

God answered me, *"This is just where I want you."* God always arranges for us to be in a wilderness alone. Just when you think He's all you have, you will find He's all you need.

During this time God also described to me the magnitude of satan's plan to destroy my life. I was on the devil's hit list in the number-one spot. My thoughts turned over and over, *What a great work God has for me...for satan to put forth so much effort to destroy me.*

The days and nights became a blur as I lay in that hospital bed. The drapes remained closed because light causes excruciating pain to people with meningitis. I received powerful medication, yet my mind remained clear because the light of Jesus Christ was shining in my soul. God's word to me never changed.

"Don't die in your winter. Fight with all you've got."

So I fought. I endured. I persevered, knowing that if I did not, this wonderful mission and ministry that God had for me would never come to fruition.

Then satan attacked my home. My husband, a former pastor, left the Lord. He went back to the world and no longer wanted the responsibility of a wife and his two small children. To add to this pain, I received word that my mother had been called home to be with the Lord.

It is one thing to be attacked physically, but it is another thing to have the rug pulled out from under your feet. This is what winter does. One day I was walking along and the next thing I knew, I hit a patch of ice and down I went! The breath was knocked out of me and I lay there struggling to cry, "Jesus!"

WINTER CAN BE QUIET

Sometimes in the winter, everything is still and quiet. This can be a very frightening time. I remember an old movie that portrayed the end of the world after a nuclear explosion and only one man remained alive in lonely silence. Sometimes God seems to be silent, but He is still there and is still preparing us.

Even as the heavens were silent for 400 years between the prophetic words of Malachi and the gospel story, God was still active because He was preparing the world to receive His Son.

In the natural, even though everything appears to be cold and dead, if you dig down through the snow and the dirt deep enough, you will find life. The insects, moles, and squirrels are still there. The plants are dormant, but they are alive and they will bloom again in the spring.

It is very easy to be excited during the times that you can hear God's voice clearly and audibly, but sometimes it is difficult when He appears to be silent. Anybody can praise God during the times when the power of God is manifested in a powerful way. All of Israel celebrated and praised God when they crossed the Red Sea. However, we cannot become dependent upon these manifestations and signs because, if they are not there, we begin to believe that God has left us.

During a season of intense difficulty, it sometimes seems that God is silent. It is important that you know God's voice for yourself because satan is a master at deception. He can imitate the voice of God and easily lead you astray if you have not learned to be patient and to wait on God's still, small voice. Regardless of which way the Lord asks you to go, you must understand one thing—spirits of deception lie on every side with treacherous plots to lure you away from God. Even Jesus sent His disciples out two by two with warnings about the physical and spiritual dangers of their journey.

Deception can be very subtle. It can come through well-meaning people who hurry to analyze your situation. They seem to know more about you than you do! There even may come a time when you must turn a deaf ear to everyone. So, it is your personal responsibility to learn to know God's voice for yourself. That way if the whole world tells you one thing and God tells you something else, you will have the strength and the boldness to follow God in your life.

I See People Growing Like Trees

As a pastor, I look at my congregation and I see a variety of trees. Some are old and the bark is peeling off. It is summertime in their lives, but the branches are bare and there is nothing there but death. The fact that the old trees are still standing says that there is "life" somewhere. Unless the tree has fallen over, I know that somewhere there is hope. I feed the life that is there and prune the dead branches away through preaching and teaching.

These trees stand right alongside seedlings and saplings. I see saplings that have never had that protective tubing to safeguard and encourage proper growth. They are growing bent over and distorted. As pastor, I need to go to those saplings that have been distorted because of legalism, bondage, and traditionalism. It is my job to preach and teach the Word of God so the Holy Spirit can break those distorted branches. This has to be done lovingly, in order that they will grow straight and healthy. Then, there are little seedlings that just need a real good caregiver who will prepare them to go through their spiritual seasons. "The grass withereth, the flower fadeth: but the word of our God shall stand for ever" (Is. 40:8).

As I look over the waiting congregation, I am energized. I see a potpourri of God's people. My church is always filled with a unique mix of people from all walks of life. The sister with a degree from a prestigious university sits next to a brother who lives in a homeless shelter. The lady in the choir stands next to a sister who goes home to a rehab center after service every Sunday. I see these people, and I am energized because I have just what they need—a sure word from the Lord.

When I look at them, I see what Jesus sees—lost people in search of a Savior.

GOD IS NOT SURPRISED

Whatever it is in your life, you can make it. It is not a surprise to God. Your broken marriage is not a surprise to God. Your child on drugs is not a surprise. God is not shocked when you are fired from your job. He is not "caught off guard" by anything that happens in your life. God thinks about you 24 hours a day. His Word says, "What is man, that Thou art mindful of him? and the son of man, that Thou visitest him?" (Ps. 8:4)

It is mind-boggling to me to know that, right now, this moment, God is thinking about me. When I am asleep, He is thinking about me. He is thinking about you too. Even though we must take responsibility for our own choices in life, it is a comfort to know that God can take even our bad choices and cause them to work for our good.

And we know that all things work together for good to them that love God, to them who are the called according to His purpose (Romans 8:28).

What a wonderful outlook! You cannot only make it, you can come out of it thriving and praising God for the experience. What the devil means for evil, God can turn it around for good. When He brings you out, you know that all the praise belongs to Him. Adversity brings out the best in us; therefore, we are able to rejoice when hardship comes upon us.

My brethren, count it all joy when ye fall into divers temptations; knowing this, that the trying of your faith worketh patience. But let patience have her perfect work, that ye may be perfect and entire, wanting nothing (James 1:2-4).

When we encounter adversity in life, most of us are tempted to ask God, "Why?" I have *always known why* I had to pass through the deepest, darkest valley in life. I have always understood why I had to experience a spiritual winter. *I volunteered.*

Early in my walk with the Lord, I asked Him to use me. I asked God to anoint me and make me a mighty instrument in His hand. I have never been satisfied with mediocrity in anything. So God was just answering the prayer I had prayed. The saddest moment for a believer is the moment he leaves this life without having completed the mission he was sent to do. I asked God to use me and He answered my prayer according to His own will and His own way. Yes, I volunteered.

Prepare for Winter

Many people who live in winter climates actually enjoy the season because they learn to protect themselves from its negative effects. They ski, ice skate, and sled down snowy slopes. They enjoy frosty icicles that glisten in the winter sun and find great delight in roasting marshmallows over an open fire. The cold frigid air actually *invites* vacationers. They are *prepared* for winter.

We too must be spiritually prepared to protect ourselves from the negative effects of a harsh winter. Our preparations do not stop the season from coming, but they do protect us from devastation. We need to be fully clothed in the armor of God (see Eph. 6:10-17) and the garments of salvation and praise (see Is. 61:3,10). If we are properly attired spiritually, then situations and circumstances will not affect us in a negative way.

Spring Always Follows Winter

One seasonal year passes to the next and each winter promises a new springtime. After our initial springtime in the Lord, we are ready to bloom forth and produce fruit. Each cycle of seasons gives us new strength and Christian maturity. Having passed through once, we know what to expect, how to take advantage of each season, and how to survive. We know that we are not alone. As with the tribe of Judah, God is here with us. He is always present, and always preparing us for one more seasonal change so that our roots will dig deeper in Him and we will bear fruit. "And the remnant that is escaped of the house of Judah shall yet again take root downward, and bear fruit upward" (2 Kings 19:30).

When we get to the point where we can thrive in the midst of adversity, we are like the evergreens that have learned to be majestic in every season. The seasons pass, but our branches are green. The pruning comes, but our sap is thick and sticky. We heal fast. Spring, summer, fall, or winter, our branches spread out to glorify the King of kings while we shelter others from the harsh winds of winter and offer shade from the summer heat. The fruit we bear is full of seeds, falling to the ground, and giving birth to new seedlings. "Blessed is the man...his leaf also shall not wither; and whatsoever he doeth shall prosper" (Ps. 1:1,3).

SPIRITUAL TREES NEED LIVING WATER

As the pastor and shepherd of the people, it is my responsibility to make sure that the river in the midst of the congregation contains pure, unpolluted living water so the spiritual trees can all grow strong, healthy, and vibrant.

I do this by studying and preparing myself spiritually in prayer. The way that I live my life is important because polluted water will poison my people. If I grow stagnant from an ineffective prayer life or if I fail to study to show myself approved (see 2 Tim. 2:15), then the water is there, but it is stagnant and will not refresh the people or bring cleansing.

Pastoring is not a position of power. It is a position of tremendous responsibility. It is as though God has made me a caretaker over this well of Living Water. A good water source is vital to the life and health of everything that is growing.

I must make certain that no one comes along and pollutes this well with anything that is not of God. I must make certain that it is in perfect condition—pure, and untainted for those who are thirsty. God holds me responsible. This is what ministry is all about. We are caretakers of the well of Living Water and God holds us accountable.

Every winter season has been a joy for me because the melting snow always yields more refreshing water. If we endure the winter of hardship, the Lord assures us that the springtime of His joy will far exceed our expectations.

I know that I am in my spring and that winter has passed. Blessings chase us in our spring season. They hunt us down and pick us out in a crowd. During our spiritual springtime, our cup overflows with joy until we are laughing and crying at the same time.

You cannot *afford* to die in the winter...*your season is coming*!

CHAPTER

3

HOW TO RECOGNIZE THE APPROACH OF YOUR SEASON

⟡

"To every thing there is a season, and a time to every purpose under the heaven" (Eccles. 3:1). Solomon tells us that there is a right time for everything and that God has a plan for all people. Although we face many problems that seem to contradict God's plan, these should not be barriers to believing in Him. Rather, they should be opportunities for us to discover that, without God, life's problems do not have lasting solutions.

We need to understand that God is a just God and that He appropriates or gives us opportunities to advance according to His divine purpose. Psalm 1 teaches us that the blessed man meditates on the Word while he waits. It also says that we bring forth fruit in our own season.

And he shall be like a tree planted by the rivers of water, that bringeth forth his fruit in his season; his leaf also shall not wither; and whatsoever he doeth shall prosper (Psalm 1:3).

SEASONAL PREPARATION

It is a good thing to recognize your season and prepare for it before it comes. In the natural, when we know that winter is about to come, we prepare ourselves by making sure that the furnace has enough oil, we have warm clothing to wear, and the windows and doorways of our home are properly insulated. We want to be fully prepared to handle anything that bad weather might bring.

We prepare for the hot weather of summer by making sure that the air conditioning equipment in our home is in good working order. Likewise, we must be spiritually prepared for those seasonal changes that occur in our lives.

THE SEASON'S BEST

Natural fruit will not ripen prior to its season. It is not as palatable if it is not given sufficient time to ripen. Restaurant menus have a notation that says, "Certain items can be served only when their fruit is in season." For example, it is not a good thing to order cheesecake with strawberries in the dead of winter. Although strawberries are available in winter, they are not at their peak of perfection. They are not as sweet, as red, as juicy, or as tasty as they are in the height of their season.

When our spiritual fruit comes forth in the right season, everything that we do will prosper. We will prosper because God will open the doors. God will make opportunities that can be made only when His divine hand is in our life. God's methods may change, but His ultimate purpose (that we have an intimate relationship with Him) does not.

BLESSINGS HAVE THEIR SEASON

As human beings, we usually think we need to know what comes next. God does not always make us privy to such information. However, He has promised that if we walk uprightly, He will not withhold any good thing from us.

For the Lord God is a sun and shield: the Lord will give grace and glory: no good thing will He withhold from them that walk uprightly (Psalm 84:11).

Therefore, we must conclude that if God withholds a certain thing that we have been praying for, and He does not bring it forth, then it is no longer working for our good. In other words, there are some blessings that God cannot give us because it is not the right season for that specific blessing.

We Will Be Able to Recognize the Approach

God has also promised us that we will be able to recognize the approach of seasons and know when new things are about to spring forth. "Behold, I will do a new thing; now it shall spring forth; shall ye not know it?" (Is. 43:19a)

There are three ways that we can recognize the approach of our blessed season.

1. God plants us in a stable and secure place.

2. Our inner clock is set for a divine appointment.

3. The enemy comes in like a flood.

1. God Plants Us in a Stable and Secure Place

Psalm 1 says that the blessed man does not just grow, but is also planted. We have to realize that God plants the feet of a blessed person. Never does a blessed person just pop up like a weed. He is planted at a specific time, in a specific place, to accomplish a divine purpose. "To appoint unto them...that they might be called trees of righteousness, the planting of the Lord, that He might be glorified" (Is. 61:3).

People who always move from church to church never grow well spiritually. Even a plant in the natural needs a stable, consistent, secure place to grow. Flowers thrive when they are perched near a window with a great deal of sunshine. But if they are in front of a window one day, behind a sofa the next day, on the kitchen countertop the next day, and in a closet the next day, the plants will not grow very well because they do not receive consistent light. They always have to adjust and readjust to their surroundings.

In order for us to grow well, we need a stable and consistent place. We must be planted in a Bible-believing church. After all, we grow down before we grow up. God is not concerned about how high our trunk grows; He is concerned about how deep our roots go.

In the natural, when a flower is placed in the ground, its roots reach down below the surface to anchor the plant and make it secure. The root system, therefore, is far more important to the health and viability of the plant than the beautiful flower that crowns it. If the delicate petals are cut off, a healthy root system will cause new blossoms to grow back in time.

FUNGI CHRISTIANS

There are plants called fungi, which do not have a root system. They do not have chlorophyll, so they do not need light in order to survive. A fungus simply attaches itself to the side of a tree and grows. Because it has no root system, the slightest disturbance, such as a strong wind or harsh weather, can easily dislodge it or blow it away.

If we are not part of a Bible-believing, God-loving, Christ-centered church fellowship, we are like that fungus without a root system. Every little disturbance in life uproots us and blows us away, all because we are not rooted and anchored in God.

CELEBRATE THE APPROACH!

God is preparing us to be a blessing to Him and to others. God knows that the real challenge is to produce quality and not quantity. As we recognize the approach of our season, we should celebrate what God is about to do in our life.

Even if you do not know what the future holds, you know that God has promised you certain things in His Word. So if you hold on to His promises, then God can develop the character in you that is necessary to thrive in the ministry that He calls you to.

Your heart should be thumping in your chest and your blood should be racing like a car engine, knowing that God will soon bring about a great harvest in your life.

The devil, the enemy, always knows when God is about to bless you tremendously. Sometimes the devil actually recognizes the approach of our season before we do. This is why it is so important for us to understand the seasonal nature of God. Satan watches for these changes.

We will always have seasons of struggles and testing. Sometimes everything we attempt to do will seem to go wrong. Regardless of our prayers and consecration, adversity will come. We cannot pray away God's seasons. The Lord has a purpose in appointing only certain seasons for fruitfulness.

Natural plants are not fruitful all the time. The evergreen tree seems to be in its fullest bloom all the time, but actually, it is the healthiest in the wintertime.

LIGHT AFFLICTIONS

We need seasons of struggle. These periods help to destroy our pride in our own ability. They reinforce our dependency on the sufficiency of God.

When God sends the chilly winds of winter to blow on our circumstances, we still have to trust Him. In spite of our dislike for the blinding winds and the icy grip of winter seasons, there is a purpose for these temporary inconveniences.

The apostle Paul calls these times "light afflictions," which are but for a moment (see 2 Cor. 4:17). I often tell myself,

"Whatever I'm going through, just remember that this too shall pass." If it is raining, it never rains all the time. If it is midnight, it never stays midnight forever. Morning is just around the corner.

There are some situations that we are not meant to change or alter, but only to survive and outlive them. We have to be like a tree in the frosty arms of winter. The tree silently refurbishes its strength, preparing for next season's fruitfulness. Its branches rock in the wind and the sap and the substance of the tree go underground. It is not the end.

In the spring it will push its way up to a new experience of budding. Temporary setbacks always create opportunities for fresh commitment and for renewal.

2. OUR INNER CLOCK IS SET FOR A DIVINE APPOINTMENT

God has set a predetermined appointment to bring His promises to pass in our lives. He sets the clock. Because the Holy Spirit dwells within us, though, we have an inner awareness of this appointment.

This inner awareness makes us realize that, in spite of temporary circumstances, God has a present time of deliverance. Therefore, it is God's timing that we must learn. God synchronizes His answers to accomplish His purpose.

> *In whom also we have obtained an inheritance, being predestinated according to the purpose of Him who worketh all things after the counsel of His own will (Ephesians 1:11).*

God even sets the timing for the activation of your call. You cannot activate your call without God. When it is your time to be blessed, God puts everything in order. Take, for example, the children of Israel as they escaped slavery and bondage in Egypt. At the time of their deliverance, God caused all things to work in obedience so His divine will would come to pass.

> *Also take your flocks and your herds, as ye have said, and be gone; and bless me also. ... And the children of Israel did according to the word of Moses; and they borrowed of the Egyptians jewels of silver, and jewels of gold, and raiment: and the Lord gave the people favour in the sight of the Egyptians, so that they lent unto them such things as they required. And they spoiled the Egyptians* (Exodus 12:32,35-36).

At the right time, God caused everything to work in perfect divine order. In fact, it was so much in order that the Egyptians even blessed the children of Israel as they left the bondage of Egypt. The Israelites took fine things, expensive things, gold, and silver with them.

Even so, in our lives, when we have completed a time of suffering, testing, and storms, everything seems to click and we begin to come into our best season. God sets the timing for these blessings.

THE BLESSINGS WILL COME

God will have people bless you financially. He will open doors for you. He will not only open doors, but God will cut doors out of brick walls and enable you to go through situations that, in the natural, would be impossible for you to handle. But God will bless you and cause all things to work in obedience *when it is time for Him to activate certain blessings in your life.*

There is what I call a "best time." When we look at flowers, fruits, and vegetables in the natural, there is always a "best time" for each thing growing in nature. Today, though, we are at such a level in our technological growth that we can produce any kind of flower, fruit, or vegetable 12 months out of a year by using certain kinds of lamps, artificial lighting, and the hot-house environment.

I remember the first time I had the opportunity to see beautiful, firm, and perfect tomatoes at the supermarket in the dead of winter. There was a foot of snow on the ground. As a young child, I did not understand how these beautiful tomatoes (just like the ones I had seen growing in my grandmother's garden in North Carolina), could flourish at such a difficult time of year.

I learned that many fruits and vegetables are grown in a hothouse. They are sent to market before they are fully ripe and they continue to ripen in a storage room box. Even though these tomatoes look good on the outside, the "telling" is in the eating.

There is something about a tomato that ripens in the beautiful bright sunshine of a July summer that cannot be duplicated in a hothouse situation. Although that tomato is a good tomato and can be used effectively for certain purposes, it has not been allowed to ripen to its best time. Any other time is "a time," but it is not the "best time."

ARE YOU IN A HURRY?

Many of us do not want to wait on God. We want God to hurry up and do something in our lives. The Supremes used to sing a song many, many years ago called "You Can't Hurry Love." That sounds a little funny, but when you really think about it, you cannot hurry true, committed, stable, lifelong love. It has to be developed over a period of time.

We must grow consistently, and we must grow at a rate that God has set. Therefore, God specifically designs and allows things to occur in our lives so the maximum amount of spiritual growth will take place before He activates His blessings and our call.

In nature there are plants and animals that have what we call a "dormant" time. During the dormant time it appears as if things are not growing, thriving, or flourishing. But this is really a misconception because there is growth taking place.

Even though this growth cannot readily be seen in the dormant stage, it is there. When we go through difficult situations in our lives, we do not feel that we are growing because we are so focused on the pain, stress, depression, and difficulty of the situation. Sometimes we do not realize that this very difficult situation is drawing us closer to God.

3. The Enemy Comes in Like a Flood

During difficult times we rise to the occasion and our faith is put to the test. When the enemy comes in like a flood (see Is. 59:19), we rise up, put on our spiritual armor, shine up our shield, straighten up our helmet of salvation, make sure that our feet are properly shod with the preparation of the gospel of peace, see that our sword is sharpened on both edges, and go to war (see Eph. 6:14-17).

The season when God mightily uses a person is often preceded by a tremendous attack from the enemy. Satan is not omniscient or all-knowing, but he can see and understand when a child of God will be tremendously blessed and birthed forth in a ministry.

In my own life, the devil fought me the hardest just before the greatest blessings. The blessings came after the test, the trial, and the storms.

The devil cannot read your mind, but he can see your behavior. Satan knows when you are about to be blessed. It is when you have a consistent stable prayer life; when you are learning and understanding the Word of God; and when you are living the Christian life. It is impossible for you to do all of these things and not have God bless you tremendously. These very behaviors tell satan that your season of blessing is coming.

IT IS A SPIRITUAL LAW

The enemy knows that it is impossible for you to learn, study, and live the Word of God without becoming powerfully and tremendously anointed of God to do a particular work. Satan knows the spiritual law of cause and effect.

The devil does not tempt us or try us when we are not a threat to his kingdom. But when you are a tremendous threat to satan's kingdom, he must launch an all-out attack to bring down the Kingdom of God in your life.

So he finds the areas where you are weakest. The enemy will attack you in the area of finance, in your home and personal life, in your emotional life, in your community, on your job, and in your educational pursuit. He will also speak fear to your mind.

The devil will do anything to hinder and obstruct you from stepping over into a full and wonderful season of potential in God. So you must recognize the approach of your season by recognizing that adversity is a "good" sign of blessings to come.

JESUS FACED THE FLOOD

Just before the culmination of His ministry upon earth, Jesus came under tremendous attack. Those who loved Him and walked by His side deserted Him and walked out on Him. He was railed at, persecuted, criticized, and damned by the religious leaders. Jesus went through a tremendous time of testing, trying, and persecution before He was birthed forth into the most tremendous part of His ministry.

Jesus agonized in the Garden of Gethsemane—so much so that He said to His Father, "If Thou be willing, remove this cup from Me." Then He said, "Nevertheless not My will, but Thine be done." (See Luke 22:39-44.)

In other words, in His humanness, Jesus agonized very deeply about the suffering He was to go through. But Jesus knew that He was to come into full fruition of the very purpose for which He came to this earth—to redeem mankind from sin and to establish our pathway to salvation throughout eternity.

Even so, just before we are about to come into the full fruition of what we have been sent to this earth to accomplish, the enemy comes against us in a tremendous way. It is our responsibility, our job, as a child of God, to make sure that we are fully prepared to handle the attack of the enemy.

It is at this time that our spiritual armor must be in its very best condition. This is why God has to give us a season of preparation to build up the inner man. When this tremendous attack comes, just before God is about to bring us into our best season of ministry and blessing, we will be spiritually prepared to stand in the battle and, "having done all, to stand" (Eph. 6:13b).

CHAPTER

4

A SEASON OF PAIN FOR
A SEASON OF GAIN

ॐ

We sing a song in Baptist congregations with a chorus section, "No cross, no crown." The world often says, "No pain, no gain." In our spiritual life there is always a season of pain for a season of gain. In order for us to gain a greater anointing and a deeper commitment for what God has called us to do, there must be a season of pain.

A season of pain is necessary because it produces patience and longsuffering, gives us a heart of compassion, deepens our awareness of who God is in our life, and gives us hope. It changes our focus, not so much to particular circumstances and situations, but teaches us and trains us to keep our focus on God and His power in our life.

Unfortunately, so many of these wonderful attributes can be acquired only through painful and difficult situations in our life. That, however, is just the way that God designed it.

When I encounter a ministry that is having a tremendous effect on the world for the cause of Christ, I find the person backing that ministry is always someone who has gone through some tremendous test, trial, or situation in his or her life. Coupled with any great anointing is always a tremendous season of pain.

MANY DO NOT WANT TO PAY THE PRICE

Often people want the anointing and the blessing, but not the pain, the tears, the tests, and the trials. The cost for being tremendously used of God is extremely high and there are many people who simply do not want to pay the price. There is a price to pay, a season to go through, but God has designed our lives so that the joys far outweigh the tears. Therefore, we must endure a season of pain for a season of gain.

There have been seasons and times in my life when it seemed like everything negative that could happen, did happen, and happened all at once. These times were very stressful and tearful. Even with the enormity of adversity that seemed to visit my life, I was able to keep a smile on my face. People would say, "Oh, I just don't know how you keep smiling..." My smile was genuine because the Lord had prepared me for the trials I had to endure.

I did not welcome the hardship, but considering the blessings that have come my way as a result of my endurance, I would gladly go through the pain again. I remember being in labor with my first child. I read all the childbirth manuals I could find. I prepared myself for this wonderful event by taking Lamaze classes to perfect my breathing technique, but it was not until I was in the midst of the labor itself that I really knew what it was like to face the enormity of such physical pain. Everything I read, learned, and practiced went out the window. Yet knowing the blessing, the joy, and the beauty of the child who came forth as a result of the labor, I would gladly endure the pain again.

Just as labor does not last forever, adversity in our spiritual growth does not last forever. The blessing at the end of every trial makes the pain worthwhile.

THE VALLEY OF WEEPING

I have found that God does His greatest work in the desert places of our lives. Loving God with all our heart is a truth that is becoming a reality for many believers. It is the plan of God to romance the heart of His people and evoke a new passion in their hearts for Him.

My personal journey was quite different than what I expected, but I was driven by an intense desire to reach a high place in God. Endurance plays a major role in our success in God. The word *endurance* does not conjure up warm wonderful feelings for me. It signifies withstanding hardship, affliction, and holding steady against prolonged pain and distress. Endurance makes me think of the valley of Baca.

> *Blessed is the man whose strength is in Thee; in whose heart are the ways of them. Who passing through the valley of Baca make it a well; the rain also filleth the pools* (Psalm 84:5-6).

The valley of Baca is a dry place. It is a valley of weeping, a place of pain and adversity. Yet in that place the Lord comes, saying, *"I want you to dig a well here and discover the Living Water that I have for you."*

In a difficult life situation we look to the Lord almost as if He does not know what He is talking about.

All we want to do is escape the pain and hardship. Nevertheless, God tells us, *"Hold steady and start digging."*

The very fact that God wants us to dig a well lets us know that thirst-quenching spiritual water is always available for us, but we must dig for it in God's Word and seek Him in prayer.

I have passed through many valleys of weeping. They were dry desolate places full of difficult circumstances. They were a necessary part of my spiritual journey, and I had to know

73

where the Living Water was. I have never been to a desert, but I know that water can be found every place on earth. It is just closer to the surface in some places than in others. Water is not readily seen in the desert. All we see is the sand, the heat, the dryness, and the desolation. But if we dig deep enough and long enough, there is always a stream of water somewhere. Those who persist in digging will find the greatest amount of water and their thirst will be quenched to the greatest degree.

The Lord had to take me to the desert, but He assured me through His Word that there was water there. He told me, *"Your digging will strengthen your spiritual muscles. The gain will be worth the pain for I will use you to show others how to find this Living Water."*

GOD'S PEOPLE ARE THIRSTY

The Baptist Worship Center, where I pastor, is becoming a water trough for thirsty people who are dying. Our church has become a magnet for people who have been brutalized by legalism, bondage, and traditionalism in other churches. We attract people who have attempted to find life in dry wells (other people, jobs, or ministries). They come into our church and find that the Living Water can be found only in a personal, committed, and serious relationship with Jesus Christ.

I remind the people in my church that we cannot pursue God primarily for His power and blessing, but for the relationship that we can have with Him. There is great error in seeking manifestations before seeking fellowship with our loving God.

In the midst of the pain and tears, God patiently draws us to Himself and fills our wells with the Living Water for which we thirst. Upon entering a church for the first time, you can sense a certain atmosphere in the air. When people visit The Baptist Worship Center they often make note of the warm and loving atmosphere that they feel throughout the church.

God has taken me through painful circumstances so I might understand and touch others in His name. He has led me through desert places so I will have compassion in my heart for those who are weary. He has allowed me to be thirsty so I can encourage others to keep digging in their well.

Men, women, and children all need to be led to the Lord. They need to be encouraged to keep digging for Living Water. They all need to be redirected from tangent roads that they have taken.

The Lord said to me, *"As you minister to people who are trying to find their way to Me, you must present a sure direction. It's not enough for you to have a map in your hand. You must know the way."*

My spiritual journey took me years because I had to go down some "tangent roads" to see what others were seeing and feeling. The Lord always brought me back to the main road with the map (the Word of God) in hand.

His Word and My Prayers

My prayer life has been, and still is, like a cellular phone. With it I am able to maintain an open line of communication with God as I travel on my way. My map for life is the Word of God and prayer is my direct line of communication to God.

Looking back with 20-20 hindsight, if God could put all the troubles and devastations of the world in a box and ask me to choose, I would pick out the ones that belonged to me because I passed every test.

With the help of God, I endured—not because of my own strength, but because the Mapmaker knew what He was doing. He designed the map. A mapmaker has to walk through those places first and Jesus has done this for us. He went through every little point along the way.

Mapmakers also must have a total and correct view. Jesus has done this also. The map is precise and correct. It will take us safely to the end of our journey.

Let's face it, pain is not pleasant. Prolonged pain can easily lead to depression, which is a feeling of being "stuck" in a situation. Depression renders a person mentally and emotionally unable to change her circumstances. Doctors know that depression is the greatest enemy of a patient with a chronic disease, not the disease itself.

Similarly, the threat of spiritual depression touches every believer's life. Some think only new believers struggle with this difficulty. But it does not matter where you are in ministry—whether you are a deacon, usher, choir member, youth worker, preacher, or pastor—depression can hit you especially during a season of prolonged pain or difficulty.

The point is, a believer must "hold steady" and go on, or risk being consumed by the enemy. Many references in Scripture tell of how God's own elect experienced great depression during a time of intense persecution. In First Kings 19, the prophet Elijah is found sitting under a juniper tree begging God to take his life. That's depression! Elijah was fleeing from Jezebel because he had caused the deaths of her idol-worshipping prophets. Elijah was a constant thorn in her side because he always predicted gloom and doom; and because she could not control his actions, Jezebel vowed to kill him.

Elijah experienced the depths of fatigue and discouragement just after his two great spiritual victories: the defeat of the prophets of Baal and the answered prayer for rain. To lead him out of depression, God first let Elijah rest and eat. Then He confronted him with the need to return to his mission in life—to be God's prophet. When you find yourself in a state of spiritual depression, you are not yourself. Avoid the temptation to make rash decisions. Resist the urge to run. Instead, remember you have a mission in life. You have a divine assignment.

You can bring about your own deliverance from a state of depression.

1. Practice smiling every day. A pleasant countenance frightens the devil off.

2. Understand that God sees you and knows everything you are going through.

3. Look to each day with renewed courage and strength.

4. Do something kind for someone else.

5. Sing yourself happy. The Lord's songs give the devil an earache.

6. Remind yourself that you belong to the Controller of the universe.

7. Look good! When you look good on the outside, you feel better on the inside.

KICK THE COMPLAINING HABIT

All of us battle against grumbling and complaining at one time or another. Many times the Christian life seems like an endless string of adversity, trials, and assorted problems. Those who look on the gloomy side of life find many troubles to keep them depressed. How often Job's complaint seems true:

For the thing which I greatly feared is come upon me, and that which I was afraid of is come unto me (Job 3:25).

If we consistently look for something negative to happen in life, we will find it. We live in a fallen world. But God does not want us to be like the unsaved who have no hope. "If we who are abiding in Christ have hope only in this life and that is all," said the apostle Paul, "then we are of all people most miserable and to be pitied" (see 1 Cor. 15:19). He reminds us that Christ has been raised from the dead and that we shall also be raised in His likeness (see 1 Cor. 15:20).

We have every reason to grumble and complain when our focus is on the things of this world. However, that is not God's plan for us as believers. As difficult as it may sound, we are called to be filled with joy and to be bubbling over with hope (see Rom. 15:13).

Most grumblers do not recognize their behavior as sin. They have many ways to rationalize their behavior. They call it "a gift of discernment" or an ability to see disaster before it happens. They blame it on their personality: "This is just the way I am." Yet God does not take Christians grumbling so lightly.

In times past, God took stern action against grumblers. In response to an outbreak of grumbling among the Israelites in the wilderness, "the Lord sent fiery serpents among the people, and they bit the people; and much people of Israel died" (Num. 21:6). How ironic that God used poisonous snakes to stamp out the poison of grumbling among His chosen people.

Unfortunately, our negativity does not just affect us. Complaining is like pouring poison into a stream. The flow takes the deadly substance downstream, where the water is used by others for drinking. Death and destruction are spread to other people. Our grumbling poisons others' lives.

Negativity also attracts like a magnet. Those who share a pessimistic outlook on life seem drawn to one another. Misery really does love company. Our grumbling is reinforced by others who share our negative views.

A CHOICE

Because of the influence we have on others, we are warned not to lead others into sin by our mode of life. We either build others up or we tear them down. These attitudes and the examples that we set are actually a choice. Although we may be unaware of it, we choose to be happy or sad. We either live above the trials of this world, or we allow those hardships to dictate and direct our attitudes.

In the Scriptures, our life is compared to a spring of water. Many of us need to examine our lives and see whether bitter or sweet water is coming from our fountain. God calls us to be the "sweet fragrance of Christ," that through us will spread "the fragrance of the knowledge of Christ," (see 2 Cor. 2:14-16).

We are to be righteous in both word and deed, for through Christ, we are the righteousness of God (see 2 Cor. 5:21). In stark contrast, David compares those who speak unrighteousness to slime. He says to let them be as a snail dissolving slime:

As a snail which melteth, let every one of them pass away... (Psalm 58:8).

All of us have been created social beings. We need other people. Yet that also makes us vulnerable to others, and deeply affected by their attitudes. Still, others pick up our attitudes toward life. What do we want others to see in us—the "slime" of negativity, or the fragrance of God?

CHANGE YOUR FOCUS

Ironically, the grumblers and complainers are often those who have been richly blessed in life. On the other hand, those who have passed through the fires of affliction are usually the thankful ones. David said it was good for him to be afflicted, that he might learn of God.

This is my comfort in my affliction: for Thy word hath quickened me (Psalm 119:50).

Often it takes severe affliction to lift us out of our petty complaining. It is then that God becomes a reality in our life, and we have little choice but to place all of our trust in Him, the Faithful One. Grumbling and complaining also show us where our focus is. If we constantly look to the things of this world to fulfill us, then we will have much to complain about. The things of this world can never bring peace, joy, or lasting happiness. But if we place our hope *in* and our focus *upon* eternal things, knowing that we are just sojourning in this place, then we will find the fulfillment we seek. Changing our focus is the key to overcoming the habit of complaining.

I survived the valley of pain. I am a living example of endurance. Gain is on the other side of pain. *"**Don't die in the winter....**"*

CHAPTER

5

PERSECUTION IS PREPARATION FOR A MIRACLE

ॐ

Whenever God is about to perform a miracle in your life, there will always be opposition and persecution. Satan's goal is to abort God's will in your life and he uses other people to accomplish his purpose.

He will use those who are in close proximity to you, those who have your ear, and those who are close to your heart. He will even use your family, those who are living in your home, to persecute you and discourage you.

God has plans for you. He has a measure of the anointing He wants manifested in your life. God knows your spiritual potential and He knows your limit. He will not allow you to experience adversity any longer than necessary to fulfill His purpose for you.

What a comfort it is to know that God never allows us to be overloaded with tests and trials! When I go to have my car refueled, I have learned not to overload my gas tank. I used to pump gas until the meter indicated a full tank. Then I would force a few more gallons into the tank to make sure it was filled to capacity. I learned that this is both unwise and dangerous. Even so is our growth in God.

God knows your limit. He will only allow the struggles you need to bring out your full potential as a believer. God will allow just enough of a test to bring out His best in you. The words of an old gospel hymn by Roberta Martin gives encouragement:

"...you have the joy of this assurance. The heavenly Father will always answer prayer and He knows, I am so glad He knows, He knows just how much we can bear."

PERSECUTION IS POSITIVE

Persecution or opposition from satan is good and positive because it encourages you and helps you to have your ear tuned to the voice of God. Because God often speaks in a still small voice, we are encouraged to shut the world out and quiet ourselves before Him. We also need to hear God's voice through His Word.

God can cause all persecution, all problems, all opposition, to work together for your good. "Your good" is that you are conformed to the image of Jesus.

And we know that all things work together for good to them that love God, to them who are the called according to His purpose. For whom He did foreknow, He also did predestinate to be conformed to the image of His Son... (Romans 8:28-29).

Persecution can become a tremendous blessing in your life. You can know that God is about to do something miraculous in your life by reading the signs of the times. The greatest difficulty, test, or trial is the greatest preparation for you to accomplish God's will.

EVERYTHING PRECIOUS HAS ITS PRICE

With every beautiful rose there are thorns. Likewise, with any other beautiful thing there is a price to be paid. Beautiful things are always accompanied by challenges. Everything that is precious has its price.

It costs to have a vision; it costs to have a dream and to be a pioneer. It costs to go against family, friends, public opinion, and the tradition of the elders. Religious people crucified Jesus, and the servant is not greater than the master (see Jn. 15:20). When you determine to walk closely with the Lord, you will be persecuted, misunderstood, criticized, and ostracized.

As you become intimate with God, satan fears the awesome power that is being released in you. So he will assign demons to follow you around and attempt to hinder you at every turn. The good news, though, is God's grace is sufficient in every battle. You are not destined for defeat, no matter how dark the valley gets, no matter how frightening the wilderness becomes, no matter how cold the winter feels. You are destined for victory.

Satan hates people who are full of God and who are living in intimate fellowship with Him. These people are those who have reached such a place in God that they can be cut down with cruel words and still manifest the love of God. Paul described it this way:

We are troubled on every side, yet not distressed; we are perplexed, but not in despair; persecuted, but not forsaken; cast down, but not destroyed (2 Corinthians 4:8-9).

Paul experienced persecution constantly. The wilderness for him was a very familiar place. Peter even called it a blessing!

Beloved, think it not strange concerning the fiery trial which is to try you, as though some strange thing happened unto you: but rejoice... (1 Peter 4:12-13).

We can find comfort in the safety of God's protection if we learn several things about how satan operates.

1. The more you do for God and the greater the anointing you carry, the greater will be the effort of the enemy to discourage you.

2. Satan will buffet you in any way that he can.

3. The devil does not bother those individuals who are not a threat to his kingdom of darkness.

JESUS UNDERSTOOD

Jesus understood the Father's timing and preparation. It is the quality of preparation that determines the quality of performance. Jesus never hurried. He did not begin His earthly ministry until He was 30 years old. His ministry was a brief three-and-one-half years, but His preparation time was 30 years. He was very sensitive to the seasons of His life. When His mother told Him that the people had run out of wine at the marriage of Cana, He replied, "Woman, what have I to do with thee? Mine hour is not yet come" (Jn. 2:4).

Every season has a product. Preparation time is never wasted. Think about the life of Jesus. He saw hundreds dying around Him because of sickness and disease, but His time had not come. He saw thousands warped with the traditions and legalisms of religious systems, but He was willing to take time to prepare for what He was sent to do. "Jesus increased in wisdom and stature, and in favour with God and man" (Lk. 2:52).

We all are in different seasons of growth in the Lord. Preparation time is never wasted time. When it is your season and your time to be blessed and used of God, no demon in hell can stop you. Theological debate will not be able to stand up against you. The forces of hell will not be able to prevail against you. God will open doors that no man can shut, and He will shut doors that no man can open (see Rev. 3:8).

THE EARLY CHURCH IS AN EXCELLENT EXAMPLE

The Book of Acts is an accurate and historic record of the early Church. This Book is actually a sequel to the Gospel of Luke. It is a theological book, containing living lessons and living examples of the work of the Holy Spirit.

The Book of Acts begins with the outpouring of the promised Holy Spirit. After Jesus ascended to Heaven from the Mount of Olives, some of His followers went back to Jerusalem and held a prayer meeting in the upper room in the house of John Mark's mother. Seven weeks had gone by since Jesus' death and resurrection, and the Day of Pentecost had now arrived. As the believers met that day, suddenly there was a sound like that of a mighty rushing wind, and the Bible says it filled up the place.

> *And when the day of Pentecost was fully come, they were all with one accord in one place. And suddenly there came a sound from heaven as of a rushing mighty wind, and it filled all the house where they were sitting. And there appeared unto them cloven tongues like as of fire, and it sat upon each of them* (Acts 2:1-3).

The first century believers, who carried the gospel, were Spirit-led and Spirit-filled. They proclaimed the gospel with boldness. There were no weak preachers in the Body of Christ in those days. Those who served God did so with seriousness, purpose, boldness, tenacity, and conviction. As a result, thousands responded to the gospel message and the Christian Church began to grow. The Church did not grow by its own power, nor because of its own enthusiasm. It grew as a result of the guidance and empowerment of the Holy Spirit. The Holy Spirit empowers us to be effective witnesses for Christ.

When the Holy Spirit works, we see movement, excitement, and growth. He gives us the motivation, energy, and ability to get the gospel out to the whole world. The Holy Spirit empowers us and enables us to do the work that God has called us to do.

The first century Church grew from a handful of committed followers of Jesus Christ, to a dynamic growing community of believers. However, as the Church grew, so did the persecution of God's people. Christians were persecuted by both Jews and Gentiles. But it was this persecution that caused the Church to grow even more. Persecution became a catalyst for the spread of Christianity.

PERSECUTION BRINGS CHANGE

Civil rights reform came as a result of many years of oppression suffered by African-American people. Women's rights reform came about after many years of economic deprivation and physical abuse. Children's rights are being closely examined and reformed as a result of the child abuse that exists in our society. Our society has developed in a positive way because somebody was persecuted.

PETER LEARNED ABOUT PERSECUTION

When we first meet Peter, in the Book of Matthew, he is just a plain commercial fisherman, working with his brother Andrew on a boat on the Sea of Galilee. Jesus called to Peter and his brother Andrew, saying, "Follow Me, and I will make you fishers of men" (Mt. 4:19b). The Word says that they straightway left their nets and followed Him.

Peter did not always think before he acted. He would often engage his mouth before he engaged his brain. Peter was not the most levelheaded disciple, but he was a powerful preacher. He was the first great voice of the gospel. Peter preached the Pentecost sermon and the Bible says that 3,000 souls were saved that day. What a revival that must have been. (See Acts 2:14-41.)

The Body of Christ not only grew, but also flourished. However, it did not flourish without opposition. Any great move of God is always challenged with opposition from satan. The devil's intent is to hinder the work of God. His goal is to wear down the saints with persecution so the people of God will have no desire to build up the Kingdom of God.

The infant Church was attacked from without and from within. The early Church suffered tremendous persecution. Christians were arrested and often unlawfully executed for their faith. They suffered, not only at the hands of the Gentiles, but also at the hands of many, many Jews, especially Jewish leaders, who did not embrace this new Christian religion. It was not unusual for entire families to be run out of town or massacred because they confessed Jesus Christ as Lord.

SATAN HAD A PLAN, BUT GOD HAD A BIGGER PLAN

All of this harassment and persecution caused the Church to go underground. Many of its members fled their homes and moved to other towns for fear of their lives. But they took their faith with them and, as a result, the Church grew. Satan had a plan, but God had a bigger plan. Persecution made the Church grow.

Acts 12:5 says that Peter "was kept in prison," but there was a divine interruption. The verse continues, "...prayer was made without ceasing of the church unto God for him [Peter]." The people of God prayed!

Nothing takes God by surprise. God always has somebody who will pray and seek Him. When the people of God began to pray, God began to move. When God's people pray today, God moves. God cannot walk past a praying church. He will quiet the praises in Heaven to hear the prayers of one saint.

God's mercy is drawn to our difficult situations. I do not know where folks get the idea that God runs out on us when we need Him most. God is right here in the midst of every difficult situation that we encounter. He is in our situation waiting for us to pray, to call on His name, and to seek Him. God is waiting for us to invite Him in. God will not impose Himself on our situation.

He will not intrude upon your life; you have to invite Him in. "Behold, I stand at the door, and knock: if any man hear My voice, and open the door, I will come in to him, and will sup with him, and he with Me" (Rev. 3:20).

The Church is being vexed today. We are approaching a time when the Church will endure great persecution. We are in the beginning stages of great tribulation. The devil is cutting a path of destruction within the Church and without—from the pulpit to the door, but we are just on the edge. We are on the tip of the iceberg. We are on the verge of the tribulation.

But we need to be encouraged that persecution is preparation for a miracle. Hard times usher in God's blessings. Remember, God's mercy is drawn to our difficult situations.

Persecution and hard times bring about the miraculous. Persecution gives us something to preach about. It gives us something to pray about.

THE WOMAN CAUGHT IN ADULTERY

In John 8:1-11, the woman caught in adultery was persecuted by all the people who criticized her and wanted to stone her for her sin. But this was an opportunity for Jesus to step forward, not only to save her life, but also to show her persecutors something about themselves.

THE STONING OF STEPHEN

In Acts 7 Stephen stood as a person completely committed to the things of God. His commitment found him standing against a wall being stoned to death. In a miracle, God received him into His arms in a state of total peace. This encourages us that when we face adversity, God is preparing us to receive some kind of miracle. We may not know where it is coming from or when it will take place, but we can be assured that He has a miracle waiting at the end of our trial.

Whenever we are in a state of persecution, we should not look at the persecution. We must lift our eyes to the Lord for our miracle. "I will lift up mine eyes unto the hills, from whence cometh my help. My help cometh from the Lord, which made heaven and earth" (Ps. 121:1-2).

In my own life, I have found the Word of God to be a refuge in times of adversity and persecution. God's promises have always been a sure word of encouragement in my valleys of pain and hurt. When satan tempted Jesus in the wilderness, Jesus also responded to his challenges with the sure Word of God.

God's Word is a refuge and a fortress. Read Scripture. Commit key verses to memory. These verses will serve as your battering ram against the forces of evil. Dare to speak to your problem. *The Word works.*

> *He that dwelleth in the secret place of the most High shall abide under the shadow of the Almighty. I will say of the Lord, He is my refuge and my fortress: my God; in Him will I trust* (Psalm 91:1).

GOD'S WORD CONTINUES TO CONFIRM OUR PERSECUTION

The Church is indestructible, regardless of what the enemy does. Jesus said that the gates of hell would not prevail against it (see Mt. 16:18). So we should not think it strange when persecution and hard times come upon us. If we endure, God promises a great reward.

Blessed are ye, when men shall revile you, and persecute you, and shall say all manner of evil against you falsely, for My sake. Rejoice, and be exceeding glad: for great is your reward in heaven: for so persecuted they the prophets which were before you (Matthew 5:11-12).

Struggles, strife, storms, and hard times give God an opportunity to show us who He really is. When storms rise, contrary winds begin to blow, and suffering comes, we must say with assurance that nothing will be able to "...separate us from the love of God, which is in Christ Jesus our Lord" (Rom. 8:39).

Many are my persecutors and mine enemies; yet do I not decline from Thy testimonies (Psalm 119:157).

...bless them that curse you, do good to them that hate you, and pray for them which despitefully use you, and persecute you (Matthew 5:44).

But when they persecute you in this city, flee ye into another (Matthew 10:23a).

...when affliction or persecution ariseth for the word's sake, immediately they are offended (Mark 4:17).

...If they have persecuted Me, they will also persecute you... (John 15:20).

We need to encourage ourselves knowing that persecution is preparation for a miracle. "In all these things we are more than conquerors through Him that loved us" (Rom. 8:37). Yes, we are persecuted, but we are not forsaken; we are cast down, but we are not destroyed (see 2 Cor. 4:9).

This is not the time to surrender or give up. God is about to birth you forth in your season. This is not the time to become depressed or to sing the blues.

The power of God gives us strength.

The Spirit of God gives us boldness.

The Son of God gives us health.

The saints of God give us hope.

PREPARATION IS ESSENTIAL

The parable of Matthew 25 tells the story of those who were prepared and those who were unprepared to meet the bridegroom.

Then shall the kingdom of heaven be likened unto ten virgins, which took their lamps, and went forth to meet the bridegroom. And five of them were wise, and five were foolish. They that were foolish took their lamps, and took no oil with them: but the wise took oil in their vessels with their lamps. While the bridegroom tarried, they all slumbered and slept. And at midnight there was a cry made, Behold, the bridegroom cometh; go ye out to meet him. Then all those virgins arose, and trimmed their lamps. And the foolish said unto the wise, Give us of your oil; for our lamps are gone out. But the wise answered, saying, Not so; lest there be not enough for us and you: but go ye rather to them that sell, and buy for yourselves. And while they went to buy, the bridegroom came; and they that were ready went in with him to the marriage: and the door was shut. Afterward came also the other virgins, saying, Lord, Lord, open to us. But he answered and said, Verily I say unto you, I know you not. Watch therefore, for ye know neither the day nor the hour wherein the Son of man cometh (Matthew 25:1-13).

If you want to be used of God, you must be prepared. If you miss God in your season, you will miss God's best. Yes, the seasons come and go and your season will come around again, but it will never be God's best. If God desires to prepare you for something tremendous and you miss that time of preparation, your best season will not come around again.

If you think that you can commit yourself to the Lord on the next round—a year, five years, or ten years from now, it will not happen in the same way because all things are set. When it is your season, you must go forth, despite the adversity around you.

Those five foolish virgins missed what God had for them because of their lack of preparation. If we are not prepared, it is just too late. I know that I have a short time assigned here, and that knowledge gives me courage to say and do what I must for His glory. I have no fear of what people say. I must work the works of Him who sent me while it is day (see Jn. 9:4).

KNOW WHO YOU ARE IN GOD

Knowing who we are in God is essential to preparation. Without this knowledge we react like spiritual orphans who do not have a home, provision, or privileges. There are three ways to learn about who you are in God:

1. Look at your reflection in God's divine mirror.

2. Learn what it means to be in the royal priesthood.

3. Allow the Lord to plant you in a Bible-believing church.

1. LOOK AT YOUR REFLECTION IN GOD'S DIVINE MIRROR

The Word of God tells you who you are. I laugh to myself when I think of how cave dwellers must have looked in prehistoric times—they had no mirrors! Surely the first comb was carved from bone by a Neanderthal woman who caught a glimpse of herself in a pool of water.

The Word of God is like that. The divine mirror of God shows you what you look like spiritually. It is impossible to look into the Word without beginning to see yourself clearly. In most churches Sunday morning worship service is well attended, but mid-week Bible study is not well attended. When you study the Word, you begin to see yourself—and the areas that need growth—more clearly.

As we see ourselves, we ask God, "Reveal those areas in my life where I need to grow." We need to be able to honestly say, "Lord, I accept the challenges that come with growing in You."

Growing in God is a challenge. I thank God for those challenges because they have made me what I am today. I never asked the Lord to give me a church full of religious people. I have asked Him to make my ministry effective so I can help people. One of my greatest joys is to see spiritual infants come into the church and watch them grow.

I look at my own children and marvel at their rapid growth. It seems like yesterday that I cradled them in my arms as infants. I find that same joy as I watch people come into the church, absorb the Word, and apply it to their life. They look into the mirror of the Word and they grow.

A pastor who has a heart for souls delights not so much in the building, the stained-glass windows, or the padded pews, but in seeing people grow spiritually.

2. LEARN WHAT IT MEANS TO BE A ROYAL PRIESTHOOD

You belong to the Lord and you are a part of God's Kingdom.

> *But ye are a chosen generation, a royal priesthood, an holy nation, a peculiar people; that ye should show forth the praises of Him who hath called you out of darkness into His marvellous light* (1 Peter 2:9).

Royalty entitles us to certain things. If we do not understand who we are, then we do not know what we have.

The Spirit itself beareth witness with our spirit, that we are the children of God: and if children, then heirs; heirs of God, and joint-heirs with Christ... (Romans 8:16-17).

You may be like a millionaire who does not know that he has money in the bank. His money is there, earning interest, but as long as he does not know about it, he cannot take advantage of what belongs to him. God has an inheritance available for you; you need to know about it.

3. ALLOW THE LORD TO PLANT YOU IN A BIBLE-BELIEVING CHURCH

You need to be around others who know who they are. People who live in the palace understand a life of royalty. Likewise, believers who live in the things of God understand what they are entitled to. We can be extravagant in the Spirit because we know that we have hope. It is readily available to those who believe. Healing is available because we are royalty. We are entitled.

So many people sit in churches out of tradition because they are afraid to leave the familiar. The congregation is getting bigger, but they are not growing. Having a relationship with Jesus is not about religious exercise. It is about intimacy with Him.

A BETTER TESTIMONY

Difficult times help us to prepare to minister to the needs of others. The strength we receive when we endure is a salve of healing to those who will hear our testimony. A wise man once said, "Experience is the best teacher." An even wiser woman said, "The best teacher is one who has had the experience and is willing to tell you so you can avoid the pitfalls."

People see Jesus in our lives when we overcome adversity with the power of God. We become parables of Jesus Christ to the people we meet. A greater glimpse of who God is and the power He gives to endure hardship is shown to others when we successfully weather life's storms.

As you come to understand the reason for your adversity, your journey will have greater meaning. You will learn to appreciate your sojourn there. God desires to strengthen your testimony because the words you share with others bring glory to Him.

Hurting people do not want to hear Scripture recited to them or have Bible tracts shoved in their hand. They want to know, "Have you been where I am? Have you felt what I'm feeling? If so, *how did you survive?*"

Our testimony strengthens others. But first, difficult times build strength in us. Strength produces endurance and endurance gives us a better testimony. Persecution is no longer an enemy. It is seen for what it is—preparation for a miracle.

CHAPTER

6

OPPOSITION IS GOD'S OPPORTUNITY

୬

Opposition and opportunity work hand in hand. They are married to one another. You will not find one without the other. Wherever God opens a tremendous door of opportunity and blessing, there will always be opposition from the enemy to keep you from going through it.

God opened a door for me to pastor a church. I realized that there would be a great deal of opposition because women in ministry are very few and far between. Those of us women who are pastoring churches, generally, are not pastoring in the Baptist denomination.

The enemy used those closest to me to tell me that maybe I should wait, maybe I should think about it, and maybe I should pray a little more about it. But I knew God's voice and I was bold enough to follow His leading. If He had spoken a thing, then He would not embarrass Himself by putting me out there and leaving me without the help, the anointing, and the support I needed to carry out His will for my life.

I knew this was an opportunity for me to do a tremendous work in the city of Philadelphia for the cause of Christ. But, yet, I knew it was satan's job to bring opposition to what God had called me to do.

Instead of allowing fear to overtake me, I used this opportunity to let God demonstrate His power over anything that the enemy tried to do. So I stepped out boldly on God's Word.

God has proven Himself faithful over and over again. As a result of my leadership in this congregation, many doors have been opened to other women, and they have become pastors in churches around the country.

Do Not Back Up

Opposition is not a time for us to back up, allow fear to overtake us, question God, or go back on our knees after we have heard from God. The devil always has a counterfeit for every authentic word that God speaks to our heart.

Opposition and opportunity go hand in hand, but even the opposition of the enemy can work positively in your life. Opposition will make you stand stronger and firmer in the things of God. You can allow opposition to strengthen your prayer life and cause you to search deeply and more consistently in the Word of God. What the enemy meant for evil, God can turn around and mean for good.

Hannah

First Samuel 1 describes the opposition that Hannah received from Peninnah because she was barren. It drove her to agonize in prayer. If Hannah had not sought the Lord with such deep sincerity in the temple, Eli the priest would not have come forward to grant her petition. Peninnah meant it for evil, but God meant it for good.

This is a clear example for us. Many times God will allow a person to come into your life to oppose you. That person can turn out to be the greatest blessing in your life because the adversity will drive you to God.

Joseph

Joseph received opposition from his brothers as well. He knew part of God's plan and he made the mistake of sharing it with his brothers. We must be careful with whom we share God's revelation for our life. Sometimes people will oppose you just because God desires to bless you.

Joseph encountered a great deal of opposition, but he understood that God had a tremendous plan for his life. He used opposition as an opportunity to bring him to great blessing. (See Genesis 37–50.)

Do Not Listen to Negative Reports

I faced opposition, but the Lord told me to turn a deaf ear to many of the negative things that people were saying. I was so busy raising my children, being the breadwinner in my home, and meeting the needs of the people in my church, that I did not have time to listen to negativity. Therefore, a lot of the opposition did not affect me personally.

Opposition encouraged me to strive for a greater level of excellence. I knew that I not only had to be good, but I had to be better than the best. Opposition caused me to study more, to be more sure about what and how I preached, to guard my thought life, and to make certain that I had a consistent prayer life. Opposition was my opportunity to become more intimate with God.

Learn How to Encounter Opposition

There are six things that are essential when we encounter opposition:

1. We must understand what opposition is.

2. We must ask the Lord to help us remain positive.

3. We must take a stand against the enemy.

4. We must do what God tells us to do.

5. We must pray for our enemies.

6. We must seek God in faith.

1. UNDERSTAND WHAT OPPOSITION IS

Know that opposition is a natural part of the spiritual growth process. Expectation puts one in a mode of preparation.

God is not the author of bad things. He is the giver of all good and perfect gifts (see Jas. 1:17). It is the goodness of God that leads us to repentance. God's will for us is always good. When you see opposition in your life, you must understand that God will use it to bless you. "And we know that all things work together for good to them that love God, to them who are the called according to His purpose" (Rom. 8:28).

2. ASK THE LORD TO HELP YOU REMAIN POSITIVE

Do not hold on to bitterness against the people who oppose you. Look beyond individuals. Know that it is the enemy using people to oppose you. Pray for them because they may be unaware that they are instruments of satan (see Mt. 5:44).

3. STAND AGAINST THE ENEMY

Ephesians 6:13 tells us that when we have done all we can do—stand. I am reminded of the story of Jehoshaphat in Second Chronicles when he came up against tremendous opposition. Not only did He have one nation warring against him and the children of Israel, but there were three: Moab, Ammon, and Mount Sier. They all opposed Jehoshaphat. The Lord reminded him:

> ...Be not afraid nor dismayed by reason of this great multitude; for the battle is not yours, but God's. ... Ye shall not need to fight in this battle: set yourselves, stand ye

still, and see the salvation of the Lord with you, O Judah and Jerusalem... (2 Chronicles 20:15,17).

Jehoshaphat and the people obeyed the Lord by fasting, praying, and praising their God. God then brought about victory in their lives. (See Second Chronicles 20:3-4,18-19.)

4. DO WHAT GOD TELLS YOU TO DO

You must remember that if you obey God in the midst of opposition, your victory is sure.

No weapon that is formed against thee shall prosper; and every tongue that shall rise against thee in judgment thou shalt condemn. This is the heritage of the servants of the Lord, and their righteousness is of Me, saith the Lord (Isaiah 54:17).

I know God's will for my life. I know where I have been; I know why I had to go there; and I know where I am going. There is no greater feeling of security than to be in God's will and to know His purpose for you.

5. PRAY FOR YOUR ENEMIES

Jesus calls us to non-retaliation. By loving and praying for our enemies, we can overcome evil with good. If we do so, we will be acting as true sons and daughters of God.

But I say unto you, Love your enemies, bless them that curse you, do good to them that hate you, and pray for them which despitefully use you, and persecute you (Matthew 5:44).

6. SEEK GOD IN FAITH

Since you know that opposition and opportunity go hand in hand, ask God to prepare you to receive the blessing that is sure to come. Seek God through His Word and prayer. "But without faith it is impossible to please Him: for...He is a rewarder of them that diligently seek Him" (Heb. 11:6).

If you have made a total commitment to the Lord in your life, God will give you a glimpse of the magnitude of satan's plan to keep you from being effective as His instrument. The good news is that "whatever the devil means for evil, God means for good." I have weathered the opposition and the harshness of the most bitter of winter seasons. As a result, I have a deeper appreciation of the sunshine of God's blessings—and you will too. Remember, life is 10 percent how you make it and 90 percent how you take it.

CHAPTER

7

SEASONAL TRANSITIONS

❧

In order to move from one life season to another, change must occur. Every transition encourages our spiritual wholeness and growth. This growth brings glory to God.

Even every one that is called by My name: for I have created him for My glory, I have formed him; yea, I have made him (Isaiah 43:7).

Thou art worthy, O Lord, to receive glory and honour and power: for Thou hast created all things, and for Thy pleasure they are and were created (Revelation 4:11).

Testing 1-2-3

In order to be promoted in the things of God or to come into our best season, we must go through times of tempting and testing.

Beloved, think it not strange concerning the fiery trial which is to try you, as though some strange thing happened unto you: but rejoice, inasmuch as ye are partakers of Christ's sufferings; that, when His glory shall be revealed, ye may be glad also with exceeding joy (1 Peter 4:12-13).

At every grade level in school, we usually have to submit to a test or some kind of assessment that reveals, "This is what I know. This is what I've learned. This is my preparation for the next level." We need to be able to say, "I can handle what is coming next."

Before we are promoted in God, we have to be tested. The test itself does more for us as individuals than one who administers the test. The test indicates to us how well we are prepared to go on, to move up in God, and to take on greater responsibility.

God cannot use weak-kneed people, folks who run away at the first sign of danger, who tremble, who have sweaty hands, who get teary-eyed, who are uncommitted, and who are the "here today and gone tomorrow" kind of Christian.

When you want to be blessed by God and used of God, you must go through something to prove your durability. God allows testing in our lives. These tests are not to determine our level of faith; God already knows that. He is omniscient and all-knowing, and nothing is hidden from Him. No, the test allows us to see ourselves—our real level of commitment and our spiritual maturity. Anybody can shout with joy when there is money in the bank, peace in the home, gas in the car, and food in the cupboard. Testimonies come easy when there is joy in our hearts and love in our lives.

When we want to go higher in God, we say, "All to Jesus I surrender, all to Him, I freely give. God, I just want to be used of You."

Yet when the struggles come and our heart is breaking, God wants to know if we can still sing, teach, preach, and serve through the tears. Can we do what God has called us to do when there is trouble all around us? Then, and only then, our true level of commitment and faith is revealed.

JESUS EXPERIENCED SEASONAL TRANSITION

In the third chapter of Matthew we find John baptizing Jesus. God affirms Jesus' identity, saying, "This is My beloved Son, in whom I am well pleased" (Mt. 3:17b).

Then, in the fourth chapter of Matthew, Jesus is led by the Spirit into the wilderness to be tempted of the devil (see Mt. 4:1-11). Before the healing took place, before the preaching took place, before Jesus opened blinded eyes and unstopped deaf ears, before He cast out demons and raised the dead— Jesus had to be tempted.

God was about to use His Son. So Jesus needed to demonstrate His human capacity, competency, ability, aptitude, power, efficiency, and sufficiency to do the job.

Even so, before we are birthed forth into our best season for ministry, we too must show our competency, our ability, our capacity, our aptitude, our efficiency, and our sufficiency to do the job that God has called us to do. These are shown in many ways, but one of the most pronounced ways is in how we *accept* and *handle* the seasonal transitions in our lives.

People are in different seasons. Moods change, situations change, and circumstances change. We need to be very sensitive to the changes in our lives so we can be in the proper flow of life at the proper time. Much of our ability to experience inner peace and happiness rests in our willingness to accept change.

ACCEPT AND ENCOURAGE CHANGE

Change is the very essence of life. To resist change is to work against life; it's like trying to swim against the current. When we accept change, however, and encourage it, we are in the flow of life. There are times when we feel happy and fulfilled because everything in our life is sweet; there are other times when we don't feel that way.

Even now as I write these words, I am enjoying the mountaintop. On the other hand, by the time they are read, I might feel as though I have walked through another valley because something has changed. But that is life. Life is not static; it is dynamic. It is all about change.

In fact, everything that we feel so good about today occurs because of changes that took place in the past. We initiated some of those changes. Others we resisted with all of our being.

It is difficult to leave behind the familiar past and venture into untraveled territory. So we cling to ideas, habits, and people that we should let go of. God knows about the things in our lives that need to be left behind, and when we are honest with ourselves, we know too.

Changes occur that we may not be ready to embrace. We age, a parent dies, a spouse walks out, a job is gone—and we survive. Once we make a decision to move on with our lives, the experience makes us stronger.

We need to know how to recognize certain changes that are occurring in our lives. Then, instead of working against those changes, we work with them and cry out to God, "*What is it that You want me to learn from this experience? What do You want to show me about myself through this circumstance or situation?*" This attitude puts us in the flow of our season, and makes the best of that particular time.

RADICAL CHANGE REQUIRES RADICAL COMMITMENT

You have to be radically committed to God because you are going to encounter radical and subtle opposition from satan. He tells you that you ought to do this, you ought to be here, you ought to be there.

Spiritually sensitive Christians are keenly aware of the tremendous moving and shaking that is taking place in the

Body of Christ. God is moving like He has never moved before. The status quo is being disturbed. Traditions are being challenged. Customs are being questioned. Old habits and practices are being examined. Rules and regulations in the Church, once set in granite, are coming under very close scrutiny. Change is inevitable.

Going Through the Change

Every human being goes through the stage commonly known as the "change of life." You know the signs, sister—perpetual summer, physical changes, psychological changes, and mood swings.

And the brothers? They comb their hair from the left side and the right side to cover bald spots. The false teeth, the aching bones, and the spare tire begin to appear.

These changes are natural. You will go through the change. It is not a question of *whether* you will go through it, but *how* you will go through it. This will be determined by your degree of preparedness, your knowledge of what is taking place, your psychological outlook, your mental and emotional stability, and those who stand ready to help you.

We go through a change in our spiritual life as well. At the moment of our spirit's conception, a process of growth begins. A holy union takes place between our spirit and the Spirit of Almighty God. We pass from death unto life and we become a whole new creature in Christ Jesus.

The conversion experience is much like the birthing process in the natural realm. Giving birth is very painful. Labor takes everything out of you, but the changes that take place are a necessary process. You squirm and scream and endure the pain.

Birthing a ministry is also painful. Sometimes we say, "Should I? Could I? Must I?" Some of us do not make it to delivery. We abort the whole process because we do not want to go through the painful transitions.

You can be in your third trimester, in position, and ready to be birthed forth into the Kingdom of God. Sin, fear, doubt, and a willful rejection of Christ Jesus can abort the will of God in your life. Sometimes God has to do a C-section. He has to perform emergency surgery to get you out of sin. He does this by cutting the carnality, the fear, the doubt, and the anxiety out of your life.

Some of us make it to delivery. We endure the labor pains and we are converted, born again, and called to a ministry. Others are stillborn. Some are called, but unwilling to do anything about that calling. God cuts the umbilical cord from the world and the separation from sin takes place, but there is no life. A woman can give birth without giving life. A person can be born again and live a devitalized life in Christ.

The born-again experience initiates a process of growth and maturation. Sometimes growing is painful, but you cannot stay a baby forever. Human beings cannot drink milk, suck on a pacifier, and crawl around wearing diapers forever.

God allows us to go through changes so we can grow up. Every hardship, burden, problem, pain, sickness, fear, and disappointment that comes into your life is an opportunity for you to grow.

WE GLORY IN TRIBULATION

I remember those days when I came face-to-face with the enemy. But even more so, I remember the joy that consumed me when I realized I had successfully endured my spiritual winter season. The tears and pain of adversity are sweet now because they signal greater blessings that are sure to come. Initially, it is difficult to understand what Paul means when he says, "we glory in tribulations."

*Therefore being justified by faith, we have peace with God through our Lord Jesus Christ: by whom also we have access by faith into this grace wherein we stand, and rejoice in hope of the glory of God. And not only so, but **we glory in tribulations** also: knowing that tribulation worketh patience; and patience, experience; and experience, hope: and hope maketh not ashamed; because the love of God is shed abroad in our hearts by the Holy Ghost which is given unto us* (Romans 5:1-5, emphasis added).

Suffering was the rule, rather than the exception, for first century Christians. Paul tells us that in the future we will "*become*," but until then we must "*overcome*." This means we will experience difficulties that help us grow. To boast in our sufferings means to rejoice in suffering. We rejoice in suffering, not because we like pain or deny its tragedy, but because we know God is using life's difficulties and satan's attacks to build character. The problems we encounter will develop our patience, which in turn will strengthen our character, deepen our trust in God, and give us greater confidence about the future. You probably find your patience tested in some way every day. Thank God for these opportunities to grow.

On the occasion of every birthday, I stand my two children against their bedroom door and mark a spot that shows their growth. We laugh together and marvel at the rapid increase in height that takes place in their physical stature from year to year.

Likewise, I have noted that every tearful, painful trial stands as a "spiritual growth marker" in my own life. These markers say that I have passed the tests and, as a result, have grown in wisdom and stature. I know now what it means to "glory" in my affliction. We do not have to pretend to be happy when we face pain, but we must have a positive outlook because of the "results" that the trials bring.

James, Jesus' brother and a leader in the Jerusalem church, tells us to rejoice when we encounter difficulties of any kind. "My brethren, count it all joy when ye fall into divers temptations; knowing this, that the trying of your faith worketh patience" (Jas. 1:2-3).

James does not say *"if" we face trials,* but *"when" we face them.* He assumes we will have adversities and it will be possible to profit from them. Every hardship can be turned into a time of learning.

ACCEPT YOUR DESTINY

Your life is the fulfillment of Joel 2.

And it shall come to pass afterward, that I will pour out My spirit upon all flesh; and your sons and your daughters shall prophesy, your old men shall dream dreams, your young men shall see visions: and also upon the servants and upon the handmaids in those days will I pour out My spirit (Joel 2:28-29).

Nothing in the world will stop this mighty move of the Spirit of God. Therefore, I want to serve this notice to you:

If you are frightened...

If you are losing heart...

If you will not go where God tells you to go...

If you will not do what God tells you to do...

If you will not say what God wants you to say, then God will find Himself a people *who are willing to obey Him.*

There is no excuse, because the same God who waved the waters of the earth, who cut out the ocean, who hung the sun, moon, and stars, who says, "I am that I am..."—this same God says to you," *You are the sons and daughters of Zion."* (See Exodus 3:14.)

We are God's husbandry. Peter and Paul are dead now. Andrew and James are dead now. Matthew, Mark, Luke, and John are all dead now. You and I, the sons and daughters of Zion, have now been given the call to fulfill God's purpose.

ARE YOU STILL SAYING...?

"I'm in the valley of the shadow of death."

"I'm climbin' up the rough side of the mountain."

"I've had my heart ripped out."

"I've been shipwrecked emotionally."

"I've hit rock bottom."

If you are still saying these things, do not worry; you are just "going through the spiritual changes."

When difficulties arise, we all are tempted to ask God, "Why?" This is especially true when we are living lives of faith. The wicked seem to be living the "life of Riley" and those of us who are committed believers face hell almost every day.

I am disturbed whenever I hear believers say, "Never question God." Surely God, in His infinite wisdom, can endure questions from man. James tells us that if we have questions, we should ask God. "If any of you lack wisdom, let him ask of God, that giveth to all men liberally...and it shall be given him" (Jas. 1:5).

By wisdom, James not only means knowledge, but also the ability to make wise decisions in difficult circumstances. If you need wisdom, understanding, and answers in the midst of your winter season, ask God in prayer and He will supply what you need. Believers do not have to grope in the dark, hoping to stumble upon answers. We can ask God for wisdom to guide our choices.

Wisdom means "practical discernment." It begins with respect for God, leads to right living, and results in increased ability to hear His voice. To learn God's will in any difficult situation, we must:

1. Read His Word.

2. Ask Him to show us how to obey His Word.

3. Do what He tells us to do.

A WORD OF ENCOURAGEMENT TO WOMEN

It took an Abraham to step out and trust God to make a mighty nation. But it took a Sarah to birth that Messianic nation in her womb.

It took a Mordecai to expose Haman's plan to destroy God's people, but it took an Esther to approach the king on behalf of the people, saying, "If I perish, I perish" (Esther 4:16b).

It took a Joseph to stand by his wife, who was great with child of the Holy Ghost, but it took a Mary to cradle the Rock of Ages in her womb.

It is your time, daughter of Zion. Jesus has handpicked you to serve and to be a blessing to the Body of Christ.

There are those who say, "You can't get pregnant during the change of life." But you know and I know that you can get pregnant during the change. You see, spiritually speaking, when I am preaching the gospel, I am *expecting* to birth babies in Christ Jesus. When I am witnessing, I am *expecting* God to minister to souls. I am *pregnant* with the promise of the Holy Ghost. I walk around wearing spiritual maternity clothes, which are the garments of Jesus Christ and the mantle of God.

You can reproduce and duplicate the life of Christ Jesus in others by the word of your testimony. You can birth spiritual babies when you are "going through the change." Others see you travailing and enduring. Your strength is a testimony of what God can do.

When tears stain your pillow, when your heart is breaking and your soul is travailing, remember that *He is still God*. If you can just muster up a praise, God will not let you cry too long. He will give you a handkerchief from Heaven and dry your eyes because *He is still God*.

A Sounding Brass and Tinkling Cymbal

Compassion is drawn out of us when we experience pain. We are able to empathize with others to a greater degree when we understand the hurting places in one's life. Trials soften our rough edges. Jesus was empathic. He was able to reach into the deepest places of the pain of others and weep with them. He wept at the grave of His friend Lazarus. "Jesus wept" (Jn. 11:35).

He not only wept at the loss of His friend, He also grieved at the unbelief of people. Jesus was a man of compassion. God desires to build a spirit of compassion in us. Without the trials, without the deep places of hurt in our own life, our ministry becomes mere Scripture quoting and an imitation of the genuine love that characterizes God. Without love and compassion, our spiritual walk amounts to little more than banging pans and clanging cymbals in senseless noise. Every hurt that I have experienced has opened my heart to feel the hurt of others.

Talking Loud and Saying Nothing

Satan is a busybody. He is a motormouth who constantly speaks against the promises of God. You must guard your thought life so the enemy cannot speak fear and doubt to your mind when you are going through difficulty. Guard your thought life in these ways:

1. Study the Word. The power of God drowns out satan's words of defeat.

2. Rehearse the Word. Speak it out loud so that the words will live in you.

3. Sing yourself happy. The Lord's song will bless your soul.

REMIND YOURSELF OF WHO AND WHOSE YOU ARE

Learn to encourage yourself. Bring about your own deliverance. Remind yourself who you are. Speak words of faith from the Word.

"I'm more than a conqueror through Him that loved me" (see Rom. 8:37). "Greater is He that is in me than He that is in the world" (see 1 Jn. 4:4). "But they that wait upon the Lord shall renew their strength" (Is. 40:31a). "I will bless the Lord at all times: His praise shall continually be in my mouth" (Ps. 34:1). "From the rising of the sun unto the going down of the same the Lord's name is to be praised" (Ps. 113:3). "Trust in the Lord with all thine heart; and lean not unto thine own understanding. In all thy ways acknowledge Him, and He shall direct thy paths" (Prov. 3:5-6).

UNDERSTANDING FAITH

In order to speak words of faith, you must first understand what faith is. Faith is expecting God to do what He says He will do. Believing is acting on what God has said.

First, we must be confident that God will never ask us to believe something unless He has spoken it in His Word. Second, faith is useless unless it is accompanied by believing. Faith that stands alone, without its partner, is dead faith. James 2:20 says that faith without works (corresponding action) is dead. Look at the word *faith*. Faith is a noun. A noun is the name of any person, place, or thing. It does not have any action to it.

The word *believe* is a verb. A verb is an action word. James says that faith without action is dead faith. Just as you must release your faith and believe to receive eternal life, so you must release your faith and believe to be delivered. Remember, feelings have nothing to do with believing. God is able to deliver you because His Word says so, but unless you *believe* it and *act* on it, it is dead faith.

If believing is not joined with faith, it will not go anywhere. It is important for us to stay in prayer and fellowship with God as we read His Word and believe His promises. As you listen closely to the Holy Spirit, faith will rise up in you as never before and your desires will come to pass.

Lessons in Praise

When God allows you to go through the valley of the shadow of death, and it is so dark that you cannot see your hand in front of your face, God will teach you how to praise Him. You can praise Him in spite of whatever situation comes in your life. Every valley experience offers you a lesson in praise. God's Word says that the victory is ours. We have a bumper-to-bumper warranty that says, "From the beginning of our life in Christ until we go home to be with Him, God is always with us."

It is satisfying to look back on my life and see the hand of God in every difficult situation. I never have a problem preparing my heart for praise and worship. I just allow my mind to go back over the years to see where He has brought me from and I have a "ready reason" to praise Him.

I am reminded of mother Graham in our church. She is a precious 89-year-old saint who has walked a long time in the Lord. She sings in our choir and I delight in watching her. She sings out of key, misses most of the words, sways to the beat totally out of rhythm, and has to be assisted getting on and off the choir stand. But, oh, the conviction in her voice and the sincerity of her spirit sets the church on fire. When she rises to give her testimony, the entire congregation leans forward, straining to hear every word of wisdom. She has 89 years of reasons to praise Him!

God is giving us "reasons" to praise Him. He demands that we worship Him in Spirit and in truth (see Jn. 4:23). Worship must be authentic. God is building Himself a people who will worship Him. Are you ready to praise Him when:

The job has folded?

Your money has run out?

Someone hurts you?

People hate you?

People falsely accuse you?

People reject you?

You must hang in there and not be weary in well-doing, for in due season you will reap if you faint not (see Gal. 6:9).

God's Perspective

Diamonds do not sparkle unless they are cut. Roses do not release their fragrance unless they are crushed. A seed does not take root unless it falls to the ground, and stars do not shine until the darkest hour. We need to view difficulty from God's perspective.

Problems help us, they do not hinder us.

They bless us, not burden us.

They develop us, not destroy us.

They cleanse us, not corrupt us.

They refine us, not ruin us.

They mold us, not break us.

They train us, not torture us.

There is a story about two frogs who were drowning in a pail of milk. They both had a desire to get out of their difficult situation. One frog gave up, relaxed, and drowned. The other frog fought very, very hard. He struggled and flailed his front and hind legs. Eventually the milk turned into butter. When it did, he climbed up and out and saved himself.

Seasonal transitions will come and go in our lives. Change is inevitable. Remember, it is how well we are prepared for that change that will make the difference. "Examine yourselves, whether ye be in the faith; prove your own selves..." (2 Cor. 13:5). Are you prepared:

1. To accept change in your life?

2. For radical commitment?

3. To manifest God's strength as you struggle?

4. To accept your destiny?

5. To confess, "He's still God"?

6. To keep praising God?

7. To hang in there?

8. To view difficulty from God's perspective?

9. To pray, "Thy kingdom come"?

We say it often: "Thy kingdom come, Thy will be done." Now we must have the faith to believe it for our own lives. It is time to totally surrender to God's love and let the Holy Spirit have His way with us.

CHAPTER

8

GOD'S HOLDING PATTERN

There is a season in our spiritual growth when God places us in a holding pattern. In the Book of Jonah God put Jonah in a holding pattern because He needed to speak to his heart.

Now the Lord had prepared a great fish to swallow up Jonah. And Jonah was in the belly of the fish three days and three nights (Jonah 1:17).

This story is about a man who tried to run from God. Jonah grew up hating the Assyrians and the Ninevites and feared their atrocities. God sent Jonah to preach to Nineveh because within 50 years Nineveh would become the capital of a vast empire.

Nineveh was a powerful and a very wicked city. Jonah does not say much about Nineveh. According to the Book of Nahum, though, the people of the city were known for extreme cruelty in war, idolatry, exploitation of the helpless, prostitution, and witchcraft. Yet God told Jonah, His chosen prophet, to go to Nineveh to preach repentance and mercy to the people.

Now the word of the Lord came unto Jonah the son of Amittai, saying, Arise, go to Nineveh, that great city, and cry against it; for their wickedness is come up before Me (Jonah 1:1-2).

BUT, LORD, I DON'T WANT TO GO!

Sometimes, when God calls us to a ministry, He calls us to do something that is out of the ordinary, something we really do not expect Him to do. We put God in a box and limit Him, but God might decide to do something that is totally against the tradition of mankind, or our personal mind-set, to accomplish His will in the earth.

Jonah was about to abort God's will in his life by running from God's request. He had his own preconceived ideas about what kind of city he should be sent to and what kind of people he should prophesy to.

Jonah was a *reluctant prophet* because he hated the people of Nineveh. His mission was repulsive and distasteful. We learn later in the story that his hatred was so strong that he didn't even want the people of Nineveh to receive God's mercy.

> *And God saw their* [the people of Nineveh] *works, that they turned from their evil way; and God repented of the evil, that He had said that He would do unto them; and He did it not. But it displeased Jonah exceedingly, and he was very angry* (Jonah 3:10–4:1).

He was not afraid of the people of Nineveh, but he did fear that God might bless them. The last place that Jonah wanted to go was on a missionary journey to Nineveh.

God calls every one in the Body of Christ to do a work for Him. Each believer has an assignment in the Kingdom of God. Sometimes our work for the Lord is simple, easy, and comfortable. Or it may be difficult, distasteful, time-consuming, and confining. The choice belongs to God, not us.

RUNNING IS NOT ALWAYS PHYSICAL

We can run away from God spiritually by remaining uncommitted to the work that He has called us to do. We can remain on the fringes of our church or ministry. We can allow ourselves to stagnate by running in and out of church without involvement.

Jonah thought he would do things his way. If there is something that God has told you to do, and you have decided to go your own way, God will put you in a holding pattern. You cannot go anywhere, say anything, do anything, or plan anything. You are just in a holding pattern.

It is like quicksand. The more you squirm and try to get away, the deeper you sink. When God puts you in a holding pattern, you will remain stuck there until God decides to get you out.

GOD WILL SEND A STORM

Jonah tried to run away from God. He boarded a ship in Joppa and headed for Tarshish in Spain. While on the ship, a great storm arose. Jonah knew that he had disobeyed God and that the storm was his fault. The storm raged and threatened to capsize the ship. The lives of the other men on board the boat were in danger.

Disobedience to God will often bring a storm in our lives. Even when we are not aware of it, our sin and our disobedience to God may bring danger to those around us. The other men on the ship drew straws, relying on superstition to reveal the guilty person and to see which one of them had offended the gods and caused the terrible storm.

Jonah drew the short one. So the crew threw him overboard, at his own insistence, and the storm ceased. God prepared a great fish and the fish swallowed Jonah. For three days and three nights Jonah sat inside the fish. (See Jonah 1:1-17.)

God knew that Jonah needed some time to think about what he had done and He wanted Jonah's undivided attention.

Sometimes God puts us in a holding pattern in order to get our attention.

HAVE YOU BEEN SWALLOWED UP?

Many times God will allow a painful situation or a painful circumstance in our life to "swallow us up." We can't move to the left or the right. All we can do is sit, like Jonah sat in the belly of that great fish, so God can have our undivided attention and speak to us.

Jonah was all alone. There were no friends to call, no colleagues to drop by, no books to read, no food to eat, no interferences, and no interruptions. He had plenty of time to sit, think, meditate, and pray.

When we're deep down in the midst of a difficult situation, God can talk to us. When He has our undivided attention, He can show us things about ourselves that we might not otherwise have seen.

A FEW OF GOD'S HOLDING PATTERNS

1. When you are sick in your physical body and you have prayed, but God has not healed you yet, you are in a holding pattern.

2. When you are having problems with your children and you have put them on the altar, but God has not delivered them yet, you are in a holding pattern.

3. When you have been praying for the salvation of a loved one and they have not been saved yet, you are in a holding pattern.

4. When you are in a broken relationship and you have given it over to God, but it has not been restored yet, you are in a holding pattern.

5. When the doors slam shut before you can knock on them, you are in a holding pattern.

When we are deep in the belly of a difficult situation, there are no interruptions. God has our undivided attention. All we can do is sit, think, meditate, and pray.

OBEDIENCE BRINGS BLESSINGS

Jonah thought he could get away from God and still receive God's blessings, but we cannot run from God and also expect Him to bless us.

We cannot defy God and expect Him to bless us.

We cannot disobey God and expect Him to bless us.

We cannot ignore God and expect Him to bless us.

We cannot sin against God and expect Him to bless us.

We cannot run from God, because there are no mountains that are high enough, valleys that are low enough, rivers that are wide enough, rooms that are dark enough, or places that are hidden enough from Him.

There are three things to remember when we find ourselves in a holding pattern:

1. The pattern has a purpose.

2. The pattern has a plan.

3. The pattern has a process.

1. THE PATTERN HAS A PURPOSE

Nothing happened in the life of Jonah by coincidence. When you belong to God, your life has a purpose. That purpose is to glorify God and to obey Him in all that you say and do.

Jonah's calling was not a coincidence. Neither was his journey a coincidence. The great fish was not a coincidence. These were details in the overall scheme of things for Jonah's life.

The pattern for the life of every child of God has a purpose. Because it has a purpose, every divine detail plays a part in God's design for your life.

2. The Pattern Has a Plan

The pattern not only has a purpose, but the pattern has a plan. God took Jonah on a roundabout journey. God's perfect plan was for Jonah to go directly to Nineveh and preach to the people there, but Jonah decided to head for Tarshish instead.

That was not God's plan.

That was not God's design.

That was not God's strategy.

That was not God's arrangement.

God has a blueprint for the life of every believer. Every decision we make, everything we do, and everything we say is interwoven into that design. When we go our own way, do our own thing, and do not follow His plan, God's design for our life is interrupted.

I remember being very interested in sewing as a young girl. In order for the garment to turn out like the picture on the front of the package, though, it was very important to follow the guide given in the pattern. Often I failed to take the time to read the pattern guide, think about it, and follow the instructions correctly.

I tried to make the garment myself without looking at the details outlined in the pattern. I wanted the garment completed quickly so I could wear it.

By not following the plan, I ended up prolonging the sewing process. I had to rip out seams, pull out threads, cut out hems, or restructure sleeves. Sometimes I had to start all over again. If I had followed the pattern guide in the first place, I could have saved myself a tremendous amount of time.

God's plan is not canceled for our life, but it is interrupted by our disobedience. We prolong and hinder many blessings that God has for us simply because we do not follow His plan.

When you lay tiles on a floor, you have a plan to follow. When you deviate from that plan, you have to rip up tiles and start laying the floor all over again. Following directions is not only a time-saver, but also an energy-conserver.

Jonah did not follow God's plan. He only prolonged the inevitable. God knew that Jonah would go to Nineveh sooner or later. God will always have His way in the life of a believer.

3. THE PATTERN HAS A PROCESS

Every pattern not only has a plan and a purpose, but it has a process as well. That process must run its full course. When we disobey God and stand in direct opposition to God's plan for our life, we are subject to His judgment.

But the purpose of God's judgment is not revenge; it is for correction. Disobedience sets a process of correction and discipline in motion. God had to correct Jonah with discipline by putting him in the belly of a great fish, in a holding pattern.

God was able to adjust Jonah's attitude, clean up his character, chastise his tongue, tame his temper, and improve his outlook. The purpose of God's judgment is always correction.

Every pattern has a process, but thanks be to God, the process is not permanent. When we effectively learn what God wants us to learn, God brings His judgment to an end.

We are waiting on God and God is waiting on us. We can cut God's judgment short when we effectively learn what God wants us to learn. Jonah prayed and cried out to God after three days and three nights. God heard his prayers and withdrew His judgment.

> *Then Jonah prayed unto the Lord his God out of the fish's belly, and said, I cried by reason of mine affliction unto the Lord, and He heard me; out of the belly of hell cried I, and Thou heardest my voice. ... And the Lord spake unto the fish, and it vomited out Jonah upon the dry land* (Jonah 2:1-2,10).

After Jonah prayed, repented, and agreed to do God's will, God caused the fish to spit him up on the beach. He grudgingly went to Nineveh, preached God's message, and saw the city repent.

Is God Trying to Tell You Something?

We need to understand that God is trying to tell us something—that the best is yet to come and that whatever we are going through will not last forever.

Repeat Psalm 51:10 with a repentant spirit: "Create in me a clean heart, O God; and renew a right spirit within me." Ask Him for these five things:

1. To help you.

2. To hold you.

3. To mold you.

4. To help you to hear only His voice.

5. To prepare you for what He has called you to do.

HOLDING PATTERNS DO COME TO AN END

Winter does not last forever. Spring is always just around the corner. I know that in the area of the country where I live, the East Coast of the United States, we get snowstorms that are so treacherous and difficult that we feel like winter will never end.

Many people experience bouts of depression in the middle or toward the end of winter. They are so tired of wearing heavy coats, wool hats, muffs, gloves, ski pants, boots, and other gear to protect their body from the burning cold wind. They feel as if spring will never come, even though they know that winter never lasts forever.

Elijah experienced a season of depression after having a great victory in slaying the prophets of Baal on Mount Carmel. However, a spirit of fear caused him to flee from a death threat from Jezebel. Elijah found himself in a holding pattern, sitting in fear, trembling under a juniper tree. Elijah experienced a bout of depression. Then the angel of the Lord came to minister to him (see 1 Kings 19:1-8).

When we find ourselves in a state of depression because our difficulties are overwhelming, we must remember that God will always send a word of encouragement to help us.

HOLD STEADY! YOU CANNOT LOSE IF YOU DO NOT QUIT!

When we have to endure a tremendous amount of opposition and persecution, we need to hold steady until the season changes. Jesus said, "Lo, I am with you always, even unto the end of the world" (Mt. 28:20b).

Jesus predicted: "In the world ye shall have tribulation," but then He gave us a word of encouragement by saying, "but be of good cheer; I have overcome the world" (Jn. 16:33b).

135

We need to:

1. Encourage one another until we win.

2. Never jump ship before we get to harbor.

3. Never get off the horse before the race is over.

4. Never throw in the towel before the game ends.

You cannot lose if you do not quit. The Book of James exhorts us and encourages us to hold steady. We are told that temptation will always come, but the temptation will develop our patience, our trust, and our faith in God.

> *My brethren, count it all joy when ye fall into divers temptations; knowing this, that the trying of your faith worketh patience. But let patience have her perfect work, that ye may be perfect and entire, wanting nothing* (James 1:2-4).

The scriptural basis for holding steady is in James 1:12-17. We are to endure temptation, but God does not bring the temptation. God is the giver of all good and perfect gifts. He does not bring temptation, tests, and trials in our lives; He simply uses them to develop us.

> *Blessed is the man that endureth temptation: for when he is tried, he shall receive the crown of life, which the Lord hath promised to them that love him. Let no man say when he is tempted, I am tempted of God: for God cannot be tempted with evil, neither tempteth he any man: but every man is tempted, when he is drawn away of his own lust, and enticed. Then when lust hath conceived, it bringeth forth sin: and sin, when it is finished, bringeth forth death. Do not err, my beloved brethren. Every good gift and every perfect gift is from above, and cometh down from the Father of lights, with whom is no variableness, neither shadow of turning* (James 1:12-17).

HOW STRONG ARE WE?

The devil does not bother you when you are wishy-washy, uncommitted, and straddling the fence. But when you are committed and sold out to God 100 percent, the devil will devise a plan to hold you back, to shut your mouth, and to destroy your testimony.

We all like to think of ourselves as being as strong as the tree planted by the rivers of the water in Psalm 1. Now a tree trunk can look healthy on the outside. It can look vital, strong, and mature. Its trunk can stand strong and tall, giving the appearance of a strong foundation and a secure root system.

But if a bolt of lightning comes along and strikes that tree, you will see the true nature of the inner parts of the tree. The true foundation will be exposed. If lightning strikes your life, if some kind of hardship, problem, trial, or test comes, will you be able to bear up and hold steady under the pressure?

If we break, spiritual instability is exposed. This reflects an inconsistent prayer life, a lack of true interest in the Word of God, and a weak relationship with God. This is why some seemingly strong Christians cave in when they experience a setback or a problem. They stop praying. They stop seeking the Lord. They stop coming to church. They stop fellowshipping with other saints and they look around for somebody or something to blame.

God says that these trials are not for our destruction, but these trials are for our development. He desires to bless us and use us, but He has to know that we can handle the blessings.

If you are being tested right now, it means that God has something in store for you. You have been anointed, appointed, elected, and selected. If you can take it, you can make it. But if you are not willing to go through the test, then there is no promotion in God.

The enemy does not want us to hold on. He wants us to let go and he will do everything he can to make sure that we do. We must be aware of his tactics and ready with a sure defense.

KNOW YOUR AREAS OF WEAKNESS

When a boxer enters a ring for a fight he is not really interested in the height or size of his opponent's biceps. His past record is not important at that moment. Instead, he looks for his opponent's weak area: Does he tire easily? Does he have a glass jaw? Does he have a weak left jab? Does he have an old cut that can be reopened?

Satan searches for your weak spots as well. He knows just what buttons to push and sometimes he knows them better than you do. He waits until you slack off in your prayer life and you let your guard down. He watches you tremble when a problem comes along. He sees you sleeping through church service. He sees the inch of dust collecting on your Bible. Then, he strikes!

SATAN TARGETS YOUR MIND

Satan comes in like a flood. He devises a plan to lure you back. He comes in to steal, kill, and destroy you during God's holding pattern. In the midst of the most difficult seasons of our lives, the devil talks to our mind and challenges our identity. One of his tactics is to distort our perspective by making us focus on the problem and not on God's plan for our life.

He whispers, "If you were really saved, you wouldn't be having these problems."

"If God really loved you, then your prayers would have been answered by now."

"If faith in God really worked, you'd have no problems in your life."

Satan understands the awesomeness and the power that God has invested in the human mind. Therefore, satan desires to influence your mind for evil. He knows that if he can do that, he can, in time, change your behavior also. God's Word repeatedly reminds us to resist the enemy's devices.

For to be carnally minded is death; but to be spiritually minded is life and peace. Because the carnal mind is enmity against God: for it is not subject to the law of God... (Romans 8:6-7).

Let this mind be in you, which was also in Christ Jesus: who, being in the form of God, thought it not robbery to be equal with God: but made Himself of no reputation, and took upon Him the form of a servant, and was made in the likeness of men (Philippians 2:5-7).

And be not conformed to this world: but be ye transformed by the renewing of your mind, that ye may prove what is that good, and acceptable, and perfect, will of God (Romans 12:2).

And be renewed in the spirit of your mind; and that ye put on the new man, which after God is created in righteousness and true holiness (Ephesians 4:23-24).

GOD'S WORD IS A TWO-EDGED SWORD

God's Word is a ready weapon, like a two-edged sword. This sword will jump up in your hand when you need it to fight against temptation. We need to put the Word on every situation.

For the word of God is quick, and powerful, and sharper than any twoedged sword, piercing even to the dividing asunder of soul and spirit, and of the joints and marrow, and is a discerner of the thoughts and intents of the heart (Hebrews 4:12).

God's Word makes us wise. True wisdom goes beyond amassing knowledge. It is *applying* knowledge in a life-changing way. Wisdom comes from allowing *what* God teaches us to *guide* us.

To walk safely in the woods at night, we need a light to avoid tripping over tree roots or falling into holes. In this life, we walk through a dark forest of difficulty, but the Word of God can be our light to show us the way ahead so we will not stumble as we walk. It will reveal the entangling roots of false values and misguided philosophies.

I find the Word of God phenomenal in that the more you "walk through it," the brighter the light becomes. When I became a serious student of the Bible, I wrestled with frustration as I laboriously plodded through the complicated syntax of the King James Version. I feared that my own lack of understanding would cause me to miss what God had for me. This taught me to always pray for guidance and wisdom when reading God's Word. A lofty, prestigious education is no substitute for simply asking God to illuminate your mind when studying His Word.

The best way to defeat an enemy is to know his strategy and to plan a counterattack. Knowing God's Word makes one wise to satan's tactics. "Thou through Thy commandments hast made me wiser than mine enemies..." (Ps. 119:98).

As you go through your winter season of adversity, allow God's Word to "warn you." The best defense is a good offense. Knowing what God says about the subtlety of the enemy makes you privy to satan's devices. Study the Word of God to destroy your enemy and bring his surrender.

Jesus Himself challenged satan with Deuteronomy 8:3. "...It is written, That man shall not live by bread alone, but by every word of God" (Lk. 4:4). When you come upon an intolerable situation, you can put the Word on it. You can remind yourself that greater is He who is in me than he who is in the world (see 1 Jn. 4:4). I am more than a conqueror through Him who loved me (see Rom. 8:37). "This is the day which the Lord hath made; [I] will rejoice and be glad in it" (Ps. 118:24). "The joy of the Lord is [my] strength" (Neh. 8:10b). "Be [not] weary in well doing: for in due season [I] shall reap, if [I] faint not" (Gal. 6:9b).

THE WORD IS ALSO LIKE A MIRROR

When we get up in the morning and look in the mirror, we might not like what we see, but the mirror does not lie. So we groom ourselves and do what we can to face the world.

We look untidy, so we wash and moisturize and rub and pat dry. We shave off and rub on and pluck out. We do whatever has to be done in order to face the world.

God's Word will always show us what we look like. It can prepare us to meet the challenges of everyday life if we read it early in the morning. The Word enables us to spiritually groom ourselves.

JESUS PASSED THE TEST

After (not before) Jesus passed the temptations in the wilderness, He walked on water, changed water to wine, opened blinded eyes, unstopped deaf ears, raised the dead, and cast out demons.

His glory was greater, His power was stronger, His character was holier, His name was sweeter, His thoughts were higher, His presence was closer, His promises were surer, His foundation was firmer, and His teachings were clearer. Those things happened *after* Jesus endured a time of testing, trials, and tribulation.

It is only *after* we pass the test, endure the trials, and weather the storm, that we are able to come forth and be all that God has seeded us to be.

Do Not Depend on Feelings

Jesus did not depend on His human feelings. He did not think about how He "felt." He considered God's Word. He concentrated on the joy that was set before Him (see Heb. 12:2).

We are to rejoice in spite of our feelings. The joy of the Lord is our strength (see Neh. 8:10b). We cannot predict the outcome of anything by the way we feel. Feelings are not necessarily an indication of what God is planning to do in our lives. Feelings do not always tell the truth or agree with God's Word.

Although we may feel like God is not with us, that does not mean He has left us. He did not leave Jonah in the belly of the great fish. He did not leave Jesus in the wilderness. He will never leave us or forsake us. God is forever with us and the power of the Holy Spirit gives us help whenever we call upon the Lord.

The victory has already been secured by Jesus Christ on the cross of Calvary. We need to believe in God and in His power to bless us and deliver us. Regardless of what our situation looks like, we need to believe God.

Remember, according to the Book of Revelation, we win!

CHAPTER

9

9

OUT OF SYNC—OUT OF SEASON

ॐ

Sometimes God is silent. He does not appear to be moving or answering our prayers. Even during these times, the power and presence of God are with us in a powerful way. They are often just different. Every season has a new level of preparation for us.

It is vital to know which particular season we are in. If we are "out of season," then almost everything that we put our hand to will fail. The Lord gives us a measure of anointing, and we are equipped to carry out only what God wants us to do during a particular season.

OUT OF SYNC

The beauty of a thing is not appreciated when it is presented at the wrong time or outside of its "best season." I smile when I think about a woman I saw walking down the street in a full-length ranch mink coat one Sunday morning in November. Everyone turned and looked, and even I chuckled. The coat was a furrier's work of art to be sure, but it was 80 degrees outside. We were in the midst of a wonderful Indian summer in Pennsylvania. The beauty of that wonderful coat could not be appreciated because the time of presentation was not right.

A good cook understands the importance of timing in the preparation and presentation of a good meal. After all, who wants the strawberry shortcake before the roast beef, regardless of how good it is?

The prophet Isaiah makes reference to the personal training of the Messiah from childhood. Jesus was filled with the Holy Spirit from birth, just as John the Baptist was. He also had human teachers and received the traditional Hebrew training in the Law. Yet the full manifestation of who He was, was not manifested until the appointed hour.

> *The Lord God hath given me the tongue of the learned, that I should know how to speak a word in season to him that is weary...* (Isaiah 50:4).

God the Father and the Holy Spirit bore witness to who Jesus really was—at His appointed hour, or His "best time." After this affirmation, Jesus went forward to perform a powerful earthly ministry. We can learn the importance of *timing* within God's work from the life of Jesus.

God also has a specific time set to bring us to full fruition in our work for Him. It is incumbent upon us, therefore, to discover God's divine schedule for our lives. Jesus never "jumped ahead" of Himself. Even when His mother told Him at the wedding in Cana of Galilee that they had no wine, Jesus said to her, "Woman, what have I to do with thee? Mine hour is not yet come" (Jn. 2:4).

In other words, He said, "What have I to do with you in this matter? My time for working a miracle has not come yet." Jesus wanted to wait until everyone realized that the supply was exhausted. He wanted to eliminate all doubt about the miracle.

God, in His infinite wisdom, has a *best time* to bring you out of your winter season. When your time is fully come, there will be no doubt that a miracle is being performed in your life. If your deliverance from pain and adversity is premature, someone else or something else might get the glory. God wants all the glory to go to Him.

Whenever I face trials, I remind myself that God knows where I am and He sees what I am going through. God sees you where you are *right now*. Encourage yourself in the valley.

MOVING TOO QUICKLY

Sometimes those in ministry move too quickly because the ministry appears to be "glamorous." The enemy wants to push us ahead before we are adequately prepared.

When we see a person who has a successful ministry of "soul-winning," we do not know what that person has gone through to get to that point. They have been equipped by God for that task. If we get in a hurry and move too quickly, we often find ourselves operating in an area where God has not anointed us or equipped us. We become open prey for the world, the devil, and the lusts of the flesh.

We hurry and scurry and do everything we think we need to do to minister to thousands. It is not just a matter of being eloquent. Nor is it just a matter of having enough people or even enough money. If we are not spiritually prepared, we will fall—and fall hard.

This is why ministers who reach a certain level of success often fall into sin. They do not wait for God to give them the spiritual strength and proper focus to stay on the mountain. Their focus needs to be on God, not on what they are doing.

If you are "out of season," you are not "in season." When you find yourself "out of season," you must:

1. Get on your knees.

2. Stay before the Lord.

3. Ask Him for divine direction.

4. Search the Scriptures and allow the Word of God to speak to you.

5. Ask God to show you His timing for your life.

6. Ask Him to give you a spirit of patience. We tend to want to follow our own time schedule, but we need to wait for His.

HE PREPARES US FOR EVERY GOOD WORK

When I finally stopped running from God and accepted the call to ministry that I received as a young child, I told God, "If I had stopped running in my teen years...I would be of greater service to You now. So much time has been wasted." God showed me that He has a specific way to bring us to the place that He wants us to be. He prepared me in His way and in His time.

My father in the ministry once said, "Men and women in the ministry do not really come into their own until they have acquired a certain level of wisdom. When you are in your 20's, people do not take you seriously. In your 30's you begin to realize what life is all about. It is not until you are in your 40's and 50's that you have the opportunity to look back and see life clearly. About that time people begin to respect what you have to say because your knowledge and education have married the experience and wisdom in your life."

Preachers say that there is a difference between just standing forth and preaching the Word and being a powerful preacher. When you hear a sermon that is delivered eloquently, but without the anointing and power, preachers say, "There's no blood on it." That means the person has learned the phrases and done the research, but she has not bled in that area of her life. Thus the message is less effective.

The Lord showed me that there needed to be blood on everything I said and did. I could not move ahead quickly. I needed to bleed in many areas and allow His mercy to bring healing. This can happen only as a result of living life with all its bumps and bruises, pain and lacerations.

THE TURTLE MENTALITY

Sometimes we move too slowly in God. We put off for tomorrow what must be done today. We are afraid of the reaction of others. Fear holds us back.

Jesus said, "My sheep know My voice" (see Jn. 10:1-16). We have to know the voice of God for ourselves. Then when the voices of "experts" come at us, we can discern the difference between the good intentions of other people and God's voice.

Job had well-meaning friends—Eliphaz, Bildad, and Zophar. They came to Job with good intentions, but God had to remind Job that His thoughts were far above Job's thoughts and that His ways were above Job's ways (see Job 40–42). We need to be reminded of that also. When God's voice is different from that of the crowd, we still need to step out in obedience.

Fear produces the turtle mentality in us. The Lord has given us the authority. We have to rebuke this spirit of fear and not allow it to hinder our obedience.

For God hath not given us the spirit of fear; but of power, and of love, and of a sound mind (2 Timothy 1:7).

There is no fear in love; but perfect love casteth out fear: because fear hath torment. He that feareth is not made perfect in love. We love Him, because He first loved us (1 John 4:18-19).

LIFE IS NOT AN EXPERIMENT

The steps of a good man are ordered by the Lord: and He delighteth in his way. Though he fall, he shall not be utterly cast down: for the Lord upholdeth him with His hand. I have been young, and now am old; yet have I not seen the righteous forsaken, nor his seed begging bread (Psalm 37:23-25).

Things do not *just happen* in the life of a believer. Your life is not an experiment. Your life is not a test of trial and error. After you accept Jesus Christ and are saved, God does not scramble to figure out what He is going to do with you, now that you belong to Him.

Every movement of your life is prepared and established by God Almighty. The way is made clear. This does not mean that we live in a robotic existence or that our life is predestined without regard to our personal choices or our own will.

What it does mean is that the very act of giving your life over to God puts Him in charge. It is like saying, "Lord, I used to do my own thing, with little regard for anything or anybody. I did what I wanted to. I went where I wanted to go, when I wanted to go, and I stayed as long as I wanted to stay. But now that I'm saved, Lord, I put You in charge. It's no longer my will, but Your will be done."

Teach me to do Thy will; for Thou art my God: Thy spirit is good, lead me into the land of uprightness (Psalm 143:10).

You see, it is not enough to accept Jesus Christ as Savior. We must also make Him Lord. Making Christ Lord involves making Him the ruler and controller of our life. We yield, surrender, relinquish, give up, and give over our own desires so God's will becomes our will. "I delight to do Thy will, O my God: yea, Thy law is within my heart" (Ps. 40:8).

For those who dislike any kind of control in their life, this is not an easy thing to do. But the moment you ask Jesus to come into your life, God puts a plan into action. He has a design, a blueprint, and an agenda for your life. The Holy Ghost gets right on the job and sets the plan in motion. Yes, you might veer off the path or lose direction. You might go off on a tangent, or find yourself temporarily diverted, sidetracked, or detained. But, by and by, God will intervene in every situation and set your feet on the right course.

HIS PLAN INCLUDES "ALL THINGS"

God examines our situation and says, "I'm going to make it part of My plan." This does not mean that God's plan is canceled out or that His plan changes. It simply means that anything and everything that happens to you, from the moment you accept Christ until the moment you die, God will work it out for your good. Paul tells us this in Romans.

And we know that all things work together for good to them that love God, to them who are the called according to His purpose (Romans 8:28).

God says, "The child you had out of wedlock...I have seen your repentant heart. I can work this out to be a blessing in My plan."

"You were fired from a job, but don't be discouraged. I can work that out together for your good."

"Pick your head up because I can turn that drug problem around. It will be a part of your testimony."

"Sickness...physical weakness...broken heart...disappointment? Be encouraged, I will work them out for your good. I can show you how to use every part of your life for My glory."

God allows us to go through situations in our own lives because we need substance to our testimony. If you never had a problem, how would you know that God could solve them? We are permitted to go through certain tests and certain situations so God can build a testimony in us. Then we can go to someone else who needs a word of encouragement.

I have discovered that when I follow Jesus in my everyday life as a pastor, people meet Jesus through my life. This is not a new idea. It is a simple observation—and perhaps the most basic principle of evangelism. We lead people to Christ through living simple lives of faith.

My depth of love and compassion has grown as a result of my winter seasons. As I look back, I can see God's hand weaving the tapestry of my life. Everything, good and bad, is part of the intricate design that results in the beautiful mosaic of a life totally committed to Him.

WHERE ARE YOU, GOD?

Although God will never leave us or forsake us (see Heb. 13:5), sometimes we "feel" like He does. Have you ever been so discouraged that you wanted to quit? We are tempted to give up, compelled to surrender, driven to our wits' end, and almost persuaded to forsake it all.

The burdens seem unbearable.

The crisis seems uncontrollable.

The enemy seems unconquerable.

The demand seems unreasonable.

The pitfalls seem unavoidable.

We may "feel" like evil has the upper hand, but remember, God is in control of everything! God is sovereign! The Lord is our helper, and we will not fear (see Heb. 13:6).

HE IS OFTEN THE GOD OF DIVINE DELAY

Jesus is Lord. He reigns over all human activity. Our "feelings" do not change this eternal truth. Hypocrites cannot change this blessed reality. Sinners cannot change this holy mandate. Jesus is Lord.

Even in the face of divine delay, God is in control. He is working out His plan for you. Never lose hope—God will overcome evil. Yes, we live in a sinful and fallen world, and as long as this world exists there will be evil to contend with. But this is not the time to give into the temptations and pressures around us. It is just for a season.

This is not the time to backslide into the sinful ways of life, just because we are discouraged. Earthquakes may shake the foundations of our security. Tornados may blow away a lifetime of precious memories. A drunken driver may claim the life of innocent victims. Bombings, murders, and natural disasters may come. But through it all, God is sovereign and He is always in control. He is working out His plan for the nations and for us.

The Book of Daniel centers around the truth of God's sovereignty. This is an inspiring example of how to live a faithful life in a sinful world. As a young Jewish boy, Daniel had been taken captive from Jerusalem and carried off to Babylon.

Many Jews already lived in Babylon, a nation polluted with wickedness and idolatry. Throughout Scripture the word *Babylon* is synonymous with wickedness. This young boy had to live in the midst of sin and degradation. Yet he never allowed his environment to alter his commitment to God.

The name Daniel means, "God is my judge," but Nebuchadnezzar changed his name to Belteshazzar, which means "He whom Baal favors." Baal was a Babylonian god.

The Jews were forced to become a part of the sinful culture around them, but Daniel remained true to his God. Throughout his captivity, which spanned some 70 years, he never compromised his faith. He served the government through four ungodly rulers, yet he never yielded to the idolatry. Daniel was true to God and faithful in prayer. He could have lost hope and given up in a difficult winter season, but because Daniel was faithful to God, God was faithful to him.

GOD IS FAITHFUL

When we are faithful to the Lord, God is faithful to us. He gives us power and strength to endure our tests and our trials. His peace helps us to go through the opposition and the persecution that the enemy brings upon us.

God delivered Daniel from prison, from a den of lions, and from enemies who hated him and sought to kill him. God was always faithful in Daniel's life. Throughout Daniel's captivity, God gave encouragement to His people through the dreams and visions of His prophets. The tenth chapter of Daniel begins the record of the final vision God sent to encourage His people in their hardship.

In this vision, God shows Daniel the protection He gives to those who belong to Him. There are angels in the invisible spiritual realm that stand ready to protect the people of God against any difficulty we have to endure. This does not mean we will not have to fight spiritual battles, but it does mean we have the forces of Heaven at our hand for every spiritual battle.

Daniel stayed before the Lord in prayer for three full weeks. He wanted to know the fate of his people. Some of the Israelites had become greatly discouraged while they were in captivity, and Daniel wanted to know the future of Israel from God's perspective.

Chapter 10 says that Daniel was standing by a river, which was Hiddekel. He lifted up his eyes "and looked, and behold a certain man clothed in linen, whose loins were girded with fine gold of Uphaz" stood before him (see Dan. 10:5).

Daniel alone saw this vision. "…The men that were with me saw not the vision" (Dan. 10:7a). Daniel fell on his face because the vision was so awesome. The man was an angel of the Lord who said unto Daniel:

…O Daniel, a man greatly beloved, understand the words that I speak unto thee, and stand upright: for unto thee am I now sent…Fear not, Daniel: for from the first day that thou didst set thine heart to understand, and to chasten thyself before thy God, thy words were heard, and I am come for thy words (Daniel 10:11-12).

In other words, he said, "Don't be discouraged, Daniel, for your request has been heard in Heaven and was answered the first day you began to fast and pray for understanding." The angel was sent to answer Daniel's prayers the very first day, but for 21 days the devil blocked his way. Although God sent a messenger to Daniel, there were powerful obstacles detaining that messenger. But Daniel faithfully continued fasting and praying, and God's messenger eventually arrived.

EVERY DELAY IS NOT A DENIAL

What does this passage of Scripture say to us? It is an example of delayed prayer. Such delays should never hinder our faith or cause us to give up. In verse 12 the angel said to Daniel, "I've come to answer the prayer that you've prayed." This tells us that the very words we utter in prayer are heard and are answered.

There are Christians who teach that our requests may not be granted, but God will give us what we need and what is best for us. In other words, they say that God will substitute something else in the place of what we ask for in prayer. Scripture does not teach this. Instead, God has promised to give us what we ask for in prayer.

> *Ask, and it shall be given you; seek, and ye shall find; knock, and it shall be opened unto you: for every one that asketh receiveth; and he that seeketh findeth; and to him that knocketh it shall be opened. ...how much more shall your Father which is in heaven give good things to them that ask Him?* (Matthew 7:7-8,11)

> *...he shall have whatsoever he saith* (Mark 11:23).

> *If ye abide in Me, and My words abide in you, ye shall ask what ye will, and it shall be done unto you* (John 15:7).

God has promised us these things. He hears us and answers us. However, He does so in His own time. There is a season for answered prayer, just as there are seasons for rain and snow.

> *For as the rain cometh down, and the snow from heaven, and returneth not thither, but watereth the earth, and maketh it bring forth and bud, that it may give seed to the sower, and bread to the eater: so shall My word be that goeth forth out of My mouth: it shall not return unto Me void, but it shall accomplish that which I please, and it shall prosper in the thing whereto I sent it* (Isaiah 55:10-11).

God does not grant every thoughtless or selfish request. To "ask in faith" means to ask with confidence that God will align our desires with His purposes.

When I counsel individuals who are suffering through some difficulty in their life, they always quote the Scriptures about prayer and how we are to "but ask" and "we shall receive." They question the Lord because He does not seem to be honoring this promise from His Word. "And all things, whatsoever ye shall ask in prayer, believing, ye shall receive" (Mt. 21:22).

"My son is on drugs. I asked You to deliver him and he is still not delivered."

"I prayed that I would be rehired. The employer hasn't called yet."

"My spouse wants a divorce. I prayed and my marriage is not restored."

"I received a terrifying diagnosis from the doctor. I asked You to heal me and I am not getting better. I am getting worse. What is the deal, Lord?"

We must understand that Jesus is not giving us a guarantee to get anything we want simply by asking Him and believing. God does not grant requests that would hurt us or violate His own nature or will.

This statement from Jesus (Mt. 21:22) is not a blank check. In order for them to be fulfilled, our requests must be in harmony with the principles of God's Kingdom. The stronger our belief, the more likely our prayers will be in God's will, and then God will be happy to grant them.

How do we stay encouraged, even when facing discouraging situations? *We learn to depend on Jesus.* How do we continue to praise Him, even though difficulties arise? *We learn to depend on Jesus.* How do we keep on keeping on, even through trials and tribulations? *We learn to depend on Jesus.*

PERSISTENCE IN PRAYER

It is His time. We need to hold on. It will not be much longer. The battle will soon be over; the course will soon be finished; and the race will soon be won. Joseph learned this lesson. He held on to God's Word.

157

Until the time that his word came: the word of the Lord tried him [Joseph]. *The king sent and loosed him; even the ruler of the people, and let him go free. He made him lord of his house, and ruler of all his substance* (Psalm 105:19-21).

When it looks like all hope is gone, set yourself in a season of praying and staying like Joseph did. When you cannot find your way, when you feel like giving up, when everybody tells you what you're doing cannot be done—pray and stay. When they laugh at you, talk about you, and walk out on you, pray and stay!

Delays are not denials. Rather, they indicate that you are not in your "due season of blessing." But your season is coming. Spring always follows winter and there is always a due season. If you hold on to what God has called you to do in this life, the Word promises that there will be a great and tremendous reaping (see Gal. 6:9).

This "reaping" is a full manifestation of the Holy Spirit in your life. God will cause people to bless your life. He will cause your gift to make room for you. God will open doors of opportunity for you. People will be blessed as you exercise your ministry. You will reap tremendous blessings if you do not grow weary during divine delays. Remember, a sturdy oak is an acorn that held its ground!

CHAPTER

10

BE NOT WEARY IN
WELL DOING

ॐ

Our "due season" is a time of tremendous blessing. As I entered my due season, things started to happen in my ministry. They were not brought about by any particular thing that I was doing; they just seemed to fall in place.

Doors seemed to open automatically. Opportunities that were not previously there became available to me. God cut a doorway through brick walls of opposition and enabled me to walk through them. God turned stumbling blocks into stepping-stones.

When I had no money to purchase a building for my church, God touched the hearts and the minds of the people. We started a building fund and money just seemed to come to us as if we were magnets. People began to join the fellowship as new converts. Everything seemed to click because I was coming forth in my due season.

I came into that season, however, only as a result of persevering through a time of persecution and opposition. God held me in a holding pattern for a time. All I could do was think, meditate, and pray.

During this holding pattern I drew very close to God—so close that I could hear His still small voice. Whenever God gave me a direction or a directive to go here and do this or do that, I moved out in the power of God with a tremendous measure of faith.

God granted me this faith during my season of testing, trying, preparation, teaching, purging, shaping, molding, and building. When I came into my due season, I was fully prepared to boldly step out and do what God told me to do.

GUARD AGAINST STAGNATION

There were many dark moments when my faith in God was sorely tested, but I refused to give up in despair. I am an optimist. I endeavor to keep my feet moving forward and my face pointed toward the sun.

Guard against stagnation. God wants us to continually grow in Him. As we go through the seasons of spiritual growth, we are to progress. To progress means to advance and improve. Spiritual stagnation hinders growth in God. Even when we are busy working in the church, exerting energy, we must make sure that our work contributes to our growth. We must always move forward.

I am reminded of a dance Michael Jackson made popular a few years ago called the "moon walk." Michael would move his arms and feet to the beat of the music. He would sweat and exert much energy, but he wasn't going anywhere. He was using every muscle in his body, but he wasn't moving forward. He just marked time, staying in one place. God will use any means necessary to keep you from becoming stagnant in your spiritual walk.

LEARN TO READ THE SIGNS

It is important to know when you are in your season. The "signs of the times" are understood through a consistent study of God's Word. When we study the Word of God, we become aware of those things that are taking place in our lives. We see and understand our own spiritual growth. There are seasons for the milk of God's Word, just as there are seasons for the meat, and we move accordingly with the season.

Calling on God during the little storms gives us a measure of faith and strength. As we pass through that little storm, we are prepared for the next storm, which prepares us for an even bigger test and a bigger storm. At each level of testing, we are consistently and constantly growing. It is important to know and understand the level of growth that we are accomplishing at a particular time so we can always be about the business of moving forward in God.

LOOK FOR THE POSITIVE

There really is some good in everything. You just have to search hard to find it. Every negative situation is not a bad situation. On the contrary, every experience is an opportunity to learn something new. Look for the positive! You really can take a lemon and make lemonade if you know the recipe. All it takes is a little creativity.

I have always been very creative and innovative in the sense that, like most women, I can take something useless and make something useful out of it. When I was in college, I had very little money. Buying books and paying tuition left me little or nothing for clothing and other things a young lady needs. So I put my creative skills to work.

Once a month I would go home and search through the many boxes of clothing my mother kept from year to year. She never threw away anything. She would always say, "Hold on to that; you never know when you might need it someday." So there were hundreds of old suits and dresses that had long passed their fashion heyday. I could take a 20-year-old outfit, cut it up, sew it here and stitch it there, and produce a designer original. I was able to make something useful out of something seemingly useless.

My senior year in college was a year when my creative skills were put to a real test. I was homecoming queen and needed a fancy gown for the coronation festivities. What was I to do? I put my mind to work. I went to a local discount department store. There I purchased a beautiful, bright yellow window curtain and went to work. When I emerged from my sewing machine, I had created a masterpiece, a virtual work of art. I called it my "curtain gown." Everyone on campus marveled at the beauty of my designer original.

The seemingly useless things in life can become useful when we put our spiritual creativity to work. Learn to look at a difficult situation from every perspective. Nothing happens by coincidence in the life of a believer. God has a plan for you. Ask God to show you a new way to view the trial you are going through. Ask Him to give you spiritual eyes to see what is not easily discernible in the natural. Every difficult situation in your life is useful and necessary for your growth in God.

LITTLE IS MUCH WHEN GOD IS IN IT

God does not always show us the big picture of what He wants to do for us and with us in our lives and ministries. It would probably frighten us because God's thoughts are always higher than our thoughts (see Isaiah 55:8-9).

We often limit our possibilities in God to what we can think and see. But God is all-powerful and He can make something out of nothing. The songwriter wrote, "Little becomes much when you place it in the Master's hands." When we put our talents, gifts, and abilities in the hand of God, He can do tremendous things with our life and ministry. We need to be emotionally, spiritually, and mentally prepared to handle a season of great and tremendous blessings.

Any kind of development requires a process. A child's development consists of seasons of curiosity, learning, and growth. A child learns many things in grade school and then earns a promotion to higher grades.

Applying education to other practical subjects prepares that student for the world of work. There is a systematic process that every student must go through as he advances in life. This is true in our spiritual lives as well.

Have You Passed the Test?

1. We must be discipled under consistent, firm, stable, and godly teaching. God's Word tells us to study to show ourselves approved unto God. We must be workmen who need not be ashamed (see 2 Tim. 2:15). The Word of God needs to be sown deep in our spirit.

2. There is a time when we are before the Lord to discover our particular area of ministry and specific calling in the Body of Christ.

3. We need a time of sitting under capable mentorship in our calling. This is where we watch an anointed role model function in a ministry.

4. Then there is a time when we birth forth fully in our own ministry to carry out what God has called us to do. I call this our "due season."

A season does not care about human opinion. A season has no respect for what a person thinks or does not think. When it is your time and your season to come forth, people can talk about you, deny your calling, refuse to license you, vote you out, call you crazy, sit you down, shut you up, and shut you out. But when it is your time and your season to come forth, nothing can stop you.

Jesus was in His due season and nothing could stop His ministry and the fulfillment of God's plan.

And Jesus returned in the power of the Spirit into Galilee: and there went out a fame of Him through all the region round about. ...And the eyes of all them that were in the synagogue were fastened on Him. And He began to say unto them, This day is this scripture fulfilled in your ears (Luke 4:14,20-21).

DISCOVER YOUR LIFE PURPOSE

We are gifts to the earth. Our task in this life is to discover our God-given gifts so we can be a blessing to others. Our due season is that particular time when our gifts come to full fruition.

The devil tries to divert our attention by using storms, trials, temptations, and tests. He wants to keep us from realizing our full potential in God. There are so many unsung songs, unwritten poems, and unpublished books in the cemetery. They lie there dead because some people died in their spiritual winter without realizing their full potential.

We have been gifted by God for a certain purpose, and it should be our life pursuit to discover our purpose and fulfill it.

We are tremendously blessed of God and we do not recognize it. We look for material things and God sends spiritual blessings. There are five ways to know that you are in your due season:

1. Your prayer seed comes to fruition.

2. You stand back and watch the power of God manifest.

3. Doors will open in your life.

4. You will be laughing at the devil.

5. Spiritual warfare becomes very subtle.

1. Your Prayer Seed Comes to Fruition

Remember that prayer you planted during your first springtime in the Lord? Perhaps you prayed something like this: "God, help me to be a mighty instrument in Your hands." Look around. If you see that you are being very effective in ministry, you know that you are in your season.

It is good to write your prayer seed down. Put it in a visible place and keep this request as a focus. Keep praying. No one reaches their season without prayer. When you see this seed coming to fruition, you know that you are in your due season.

And He spake a parable unto them to this end, that men ought always to pray, and not to faint (Luke 18:1).

Pray without ceasing. In every thing give thanks: for this is the will of God in Christ Jesus concerning you (1 Thessalonians 5:17-18).

2. Stand Back and Watch the Power of God Manifest

When you know that you are not doing anything special, but the unsaved are receiving Christ, you know that you are in your due season. I still marvel every time I see a person accept the Lord. I say to myself, *This is a person who has been saved from the grips of hell because God used me as a vessel—nothing more.* The Lord constantly reminds me, "It's not you, it's Me doing it *through you.*" His Word tells us, "But we have this treasure in earthen vessels, that the excellency of the power may be of God, and not of us" (2 Cor. 4:7).

3. Doors Will Open in Your Life

Things that need to happen will happen without your having to push, pull, and politick. You will simply stand back and watch God perform. God will bring everything and everybody that you need into your life. You will meet people, by God's design, who have just the talents that you need to carry out the work He has assigned to you.

We are tools in the hands of the Lord. Tools do not argue with the carpenter. They simply wait in the toolbox and make themselves available for the carpenter.

4. YOU WILL BE LAUGHING AT THE DEVIL

Laughter will fill your life because you will be able to look back and see God's plan. There will be a smile on your face and you will know that the victory is certain.

The joy of the Lord will be your strength (see Neh. 8:10). You will rejoice with joy unspeakable (see 1 Pet. 1:8b). You will experience His joy, and your joy will be full (see Jn. 15:11).

5. SPIRITUAL WARFARE BECOMES VERY SUBTLE

Spiritual warfare comes in a very subtle way during our due season. The devil wants us to forget the pain. In the midst of the blessing, the enemy tells us, "Look what you have accomplished. See how much you are doing for the Kingdom of God. My, what a wonderful Christian you have become. Forget the past, forget the pain, and enjoy the good life you have now."

My prayer has been, "Lord, help me to be able to call up the memories of the past. I don't ever want to forget the pain. I want to remember where I have come from and that You have brought me to this point."

Spiritually, I think it is important for us to keep the memories of our adversities fresh. If we get to the point that we forget, we desensitize ourselves. Then we cannot understand what other people in pain are feeling. We need to be able to minister to them on a deep level, to look them in the eyes, connect with their pain, and tell them, "Oh, yes, you can make it."

So we must be aware that the enemy will come in with this subtle deception. He wants us to forget where we have come from. We will not. We will give praise, thanksgiving, and glory to God for all that He has brought us through. Israel recounted the sufferings of the people and the deliverance of God from generation to generation. We should do the same.

The Seasons Will Continue to Pass

You know that there will be other winter seasons to endure, but now you know that you will survive. You are like the tree planted by living waters (see Ps. 1), bearing one ring of age after another. Soon you will look around and realize that you are huge in God. A mighty oak starts with an acorn.

God will always have a people who stand strong for Him, a remnant who love Him. I believe He is using the purging of the seasons to sift out this remnant.

And I will bring the third part through the fire, and will refine them as silver is refined, and will try them as gold is tried: they shall call on My name, and I will hear them: I will say, It is My people: and they shall say, The Lord is my God (Zechariah 13:9).

CHAPTER

11

11

IN DUE SEASON

❧

SHOWERS OF BLESSINGS

In Chapter 1 of this book I described how I stood in my pulpit, exhausted, overworked, and stressed out. But I remember that day with sweetness now because my winter season has passed. Winter will come again, as all seasons do, but I know how to prepare myself now. I can recognize winter's approach.

Now I can nurture and shepherd those 14 new converts who gave their heart to the Lord. When their winter season arrives, I am ready to go with them and minister hope in the midst of adversity.

The words of my testimony have life. Flesh and bone cling to every sermon I preach. Dead people need a Living Word. The blood of Christ gives every word life, and so the message lives.

I have entered a season of continuous praise for what God has done in my life. Others have died in winter. They lie frozen, cold, and stiff in the chilly winds of adversity. They gave up. But I endured and I survived. Today I thrive in the midst of God's blessings. The smile on my face is genuine. The love in my heart is sincere. The excitement with which I serve God is real.

I have endured my winter.

I have survived the wilderness.

I have come out of the valley.

This book has been the story of my sojourn there. Perhaps God has sent me to search for you and to encourage you during your winter season.

Suffering in and of itself is not a privilege. However, when we suffer as a result of faithfully representing Christ, we know that our message and example have an effect and that God considers us worthy to represent Him. Suffering for our faith does not mean we have done something wrong. In fact, the opposite is often true—it verifies that we have been faithful.

Finally, this book is an Ebenezer. The Bible says that Samuel took a stone and set it up between Mizpah and Shen. He named it Ebenezer, saying, "Hitherto hath the Lord helped us" (1 Sam. 7:12b).

This was a common practice in early Israel. The patriarchs piled up rocks to mark where the Lord had met them. They made altars and thanked God for what He had done for them. Afterward, when they walked by the rock piles on their pilgrimages, the rocks served as reminders of God's faithfulness.

This book is a pile of rocks, declaring that God has helped me in my wilderness walk. I marvel at the faithfulness of God. I greet each new day with anticipation. Every morning I look in the mirror and speak to the strong, confident, secure woman smiling back at me and say, "*You go, girl!*" and the Spirit of the Lord says, "*Yes, you go!*"

STIR UP YOUR SPIRIT

The following pages contain words of wisdom for you. These thoughts will "stir up" your spirit and help you to hear what the Lord is saying in your life. They are intended to provoke your prayers and to focus your heart in the right direction.

I recommend that you read this chapter through at least once and then read one thought a day, during your devotions, for 30 days. Spend the next 30 days praying and meditating on the seasons in your life.

Remember, preparation is the key. Those who are prepared will be able to endure the winter.

Day 1

I live in God's time, not my own. God lives in eternity. He has no beginning and no end (see Rev. 22:13). He always was, is, and shall be. Time is only a piece of eternity, just as a slice of an apple pie is a piece of the whole pie.

Time is limited by its boundaries. My life is limited by time. I have a beginning and an end. I live in the slice and God lives in the pie.

I can see only my space of time. God sees my eternal existence and He operates according to the limitless expanse of eternity. Therefore, God's will for my life will bless me and benefit me for eternity. God has looked ahead. He has an eternal plan. His plan may not seem to be in my best interest for the moment, but God is least concerned about the moment. God lives in eternity.

Day 2

Israel suffered many hardships and persecution. God's people often felt alone and deserted by God, but He knew that His people had to be prepared to live in total dependence upon Him. He took Israel through seasons of change and growth.

Hardships and problems teach me to depend upon God. Strife causes me to focus my attention on God. God has arranged the seasons in my spiritual life in order to produce Christlike character in me (see Jas. 1:2-4).

DAY 3

Some seasons are longer than others according to the level of strength and commitment that God wants to build in me. Am I willing to endure the long winter? (See James 1:12.)

DAY 4

God made provision for Israel in the wilderness. When my season of hardship and persecution is long and difficult, God always makes provision for me. One of His covenant names is "Jehovah Jireh." It means "the God who supplies our needs." I am thankful for His provision (see Phil. 4:19).

DAY 5

God orders and directs my steps because I have asked Him to. Psalm 37:23 says, "The steps of a good man are ordered by the Lord: and He delighteth in his way." Although I do not always know where I am going, I know who is leading me there.

DAY 6

Sometimes I want to skip certain steps of my growth. I want to do as much as I can for God, as quickly as I can. However, I cannot grow faster than God permits. I cannot rush God (see 2 Pet. 3:8).

DAY 7

I remember when I was a small child. I know what it is like to grow physically, to learn, and to develop into a mature adult. Likewise, I do not want to remain a spiritual child. I am willing to grow, to learn, and to develop in the things of God. I know this will take time; God has time; therefore, I have time (see 1 Cor. 13:11).

Day 8

Sometimes I still act like a child. I want my own way. I want to say "no." I manipulate others with my emotions. I know that there are areas in my life that need further growth. I have to decide. Do I want to grow up? (See Hebrews 5:12-13.)

Day 9

God wants me to grow to spiritual maturity; therefore, He is taking me through seasons to bring me to the place of maturity in Him (see Eph. 4:13-15).

Day 10

When I reach the time that I am ready to "blossom forth" in my work for Him, I must move out or I will miss my best season. (See John 9:4.)

Day 11

An apple tree can blossom forth at any season of the calendar year if it is kept in a hothouse (protected from storms, insects, and cold temperatures), but that is not the way God intended for apple trees to grow. God does not want to keep me in a Christian "hothouse." He plants me where I am able to experience the natural conditions of life (see 2 Pet. 3:18).

Day 12

God has arranged the physical world so that flowers can show forth their best in the spring and summer. Corn and wheat show forth their best in the fall. Evergreens are beautiful in the winter. Every area of nature has a season in which it can show forth its best. So do I. (See Ephesians 2:10.)

Day 13

God has planned a special season for me. It will be a time when He can use me for His glory. His love will shine through me in a special way. I am anxious for this season, but I am willing to wait. I want to be like the rose that is ready to burst into bloom. I do not want to be a rosebud that dries up because it is not ready for the sunshine. (See Ecclesiastes 3:11a.)

Day 14

I need to know the "signs of the seasons" so I can have the mind of God and use each season for maximum growth. Therefore, I must begin to pay attention to the circumstances and changes in my life from a bibilical perspective. (See Ephesians 4:23.)

Day 15

God directs the timing of all nature. The flowers bloom in His time. The trees drop their leaves in His time. The planets readjust themselves in His time. God directs the timing of all things in my life as well. (See Ecclesiastes 3:1.)

Day 16

A hothouse tomato is not as red, juicy, and palatable as a tomato grown in the warm July sunshine. A hothouse rose cannot compare with the regal beauty of a garden rose. I can create artificial conditions in my life if I want to. Do I really want to? (See Titus 3:8.)

Day 17

If I am not aware of the seasons of growth and the qualities that God wants to produce in me, I will begin to create artificial qualities that do not have substance or depth. I will end up with surface strength, superficial wisdom, and a shallow character. (See John 15:4.)

Day 18

If my life lacks depth and wisdom, my ministry will be ineffective. It will not change lives because my own life has not yet been fully changed. (See John 14:15.)

Day 19

God is not finished with me yet. I must allow Him to continue to work on me according to His own schedule. If I do not, I will find myself walking and operating in areas that I am totally unprepared for. (See John 15:5.)

Day 20

There is great value in abiding in Jesus (see Jn. 15). If I abide in Him, then I will act like Him, look like Him, and love like Him. He is the Vine. I am a branch that looks like it belongs to the Vine.

Day 21

I know that I will prosper, regardless of the season. God has prosperity reserved for me. He gives me all that I need, regardless of the circumstances in my life (see Phil. 4:19).

Day 22

I will not allow the enemy to have a foothold in my life. He has no power over me. God has not given me a spirit of fear. I have a sound mind. I have power. I have love. I have self-control. (See 2 Tim. 1:7.)

Day 23

I will praise God at all times and give Him thanks, for this is His will concerning me (see 1 Thess. 5:18). I will not allow the enemy to buffet my life with self-pity. He is an empty mist that has no power over me.

DAY 24

God's Word is profitable for me. It equips me for every good work and trains me in righteousness (see 2 Tim. 3:16). My growth is dependent upon the Word of God in me. I rely on His Word in every season.

DAY 25

I am dressed in garments of salvation and praise. The full armor of God covers me and protects me from the evil one. I am prepared to stand in the evil day (see Eph. 6:10-17).

DAY 26

Seasons of pain are for my gain. Those who want God to use them must pay a high price. God has designed situations in my life so the joys far outweigh the tears, the pain, the tests, and the trials. I can endure this season because I know that spring is coming. (See Psalm 34:19.)

DAY 27

Instead of allowing fear to overtake me, I will use this opportunity to let God demonstrate His power over anything the enemy tries to do to me. Opposition is God's opportunity in my life. (See 2 Tim. 1:2.)

DAY 28

Changes have taken place in my life that are difficult to embrace and accept. Yet I know that I must move on. I must keep growing. Every experience in my life is helping me to discover my divine potential and life purpose. (See 2 Tim. 1:9.)

DAY 29

I want to be like a tree planted by the waters. I will not walk in the counsel of the ungodly or stand in the way of sinners. I refuse to sit with the scornful.

My delight is in God's Word. I will meditate on it day and night. I will bring forth fruit in my season. My leaf will not wither and whatever I do will prosper. (See Psalm 1.)

Day 30

I am not afraid of the winter.

I refuse to die.

I know that spring is coming.

I hear the birds chirping.

I hear the bees buzzing.

The sun is beginning to beam down on my head.

I refuse to die because I know my season is coming.

CHAPTER

12

GOD'S WEATHER CHANNEL

~

Tuning in to Divine Guidance

God's Word provides food for thought and sustenance for living. Knowing the Word gives us guidance through the seasons of life. Every verse offers spiritual insight to the one who prayerfully searches and uncovers truths, truths that bring comfort and understanding during a season of adversity.

Just as we prepare ourselves for seasonal changes in the natural, we must also clothe ourselves in the righteousness of God's Word during seasonal changes. So commit such passages to memory. These truths will bless you in your season, even as they have helped me. Be encouraged as you tune in to God's divine weather channel. And *Don't Die in the Winter...Your Season Is Coming!*

Spring Season

VISIBILITY

Neither give place to the devil (Ephesians 4:27).

THE FORECAST

This is the day which the Lord hath made; we will rejoice and be glad in it (Psalm 118:24).

185

SHOWERS OF BLESSINGS

...if I will not open you the windows of heaven, and pour you out a blessing, that there shall not be room enough to receive it. And I will rebuke the devourer for your sakes... (Malachi 3:10-11).

And all these blessings shall come on thee, and overtake thee, if thou shalt hearken unto the voice of the Lord thy God. ... And the Lord shall make thee the head, and not the tail; and thou shalt be above only, and thou shalt not be beneath; if that thou hearken unto the commandments of the Lord thy God, which I command thee this day, to observe and to do them (Deuteronomy 28:2,13).

SUMMER SEASON

SUNRISE|SUNSET

For from the rising of the sun even unto the going down of the same My name shall be great... (Malachi 1:11).

WEATHER WISDOM

The steps of a good man are ordered by the Lord: and He delighteth in his way. Though he fall, he shall not be utterly cast down: for the Lord upholdeth him with His hand (Psalm 37:23-24).

Teach me, O Lord, the way of Thy statutes; and I shall keep it unto the end. Give me understanding, and I shall keep Thy law; yea, I shall observe it with my whole heart (Psalm 119:33-34).

HEAT WAVE

We are troubled on every side, yet not distressed; we are perplexed, but not in despair; persecuted, but not forsaken; cast down, but not destroyed (2 Corinthians 4:8-9).

FALL SEASON

TODAY'S OUTLOOK

For the eyes of the Lord run to and fro thoughout the whole earth, to show Himself strong in the behalf of them whose heart is perfect toward Him... (2 Chronicles 16:9).

HIGHS AND LOWS

Therefore, my beloved brethren, be ye stedfast, unmoveable, always abounding in the work of the Lord, forasmuch as ye know that your labour is not in vain in the Lord (1 Corinthians 15:58).

ATMOSPHERIC PRESSURE

For in the time of trouble He shall hide me in His pavilion: in the secret of His tabernacle shall He hide me; He shall set me up upon a rock. And now shall mine head be lifted up above mine enemies round about me: therefore will I offer in His tabernacle sacrifices of joy; I will sing, yea, I will sing praises unto the Lord (Psalm 27:5-6).

...When the enemy shall come in like a flood, the Spirit of the Lord shall lift up a standard against him (Isaiah 59:19b).

WINTER SEASON

STORM WARNING

Be sober, be vigilant; because your adversary the devil, as a roaring lion, walketh about, seeking whom he may devour (1 Peter 5:8).

WINTRY SKIES

I will lift up mine eyes unto the hills, from whence cometh my help. My help cometh from the Lord, which made heaven and earth (Psalm 121:1-2).

WINDCHILL FACTOR

...weeping may endure for a night, but joy cometh in the morning (Psalm 30:5).

Millicent Hunter Ministries

Order Form

PRODUCTS	PRICE	QTY.	AMOUNT
BOOKS			
Crashing Satan's Party	$10.00		
Don't Die in the Winter… Your Season Is Coming	$10.00		
VIDEOTAPES			
A Ridiculous Blessing	$15.00		
A Treasure in Trash	$15.00		
Back to Your Future	$15.00		
Bent Over in the Synagogue	$15.00		
By Any Means Necessary	$15.00		
Caution! Program Subject to Change	$15.00		
Dead Man Walking	$15.00		
Going Through the Change	$15.00		
If Thou Be a Great People	$15.00		
My Water Just Broke!	$15.00		
Psyche!	$15.00		
Target Practice	$15.00		
The Devil Is Blowing Up Balloons	$15.00		
Weird People	$15.00		
You Got to Be Crazy	$15.00		
Your Attitude Is Showing	$15.00		
TOTAL FOR BOOKS AND VIDEOTAPES			

PRODUCTS	PRICE	QTY.	AMOUNT
AUDIOTAPES			
A Treasure in Trash	$5.00		
Bent Over in the Synagogue	$5.00		
By Any Means Necessary	$5.00		
Don't Die in the Winter…	$5.00		
If Thou Be a Great People	$5.00		
If You Don't Start Nothin', It Ain't Gonna Be Nothin'	$5.00		
It's a Set-up	$5.00		
Let the Daughters Live	$5.00		
My Water Just Broke!	$5.00		
Psyche!	$5.00		
Rally in the Valley	$5.00		
Show Up for the Showdown	$5.00		
Target Practice	$5.00		
This Time I Will Praise the Lord	$5.00		
Waiting to Exhale	$5.00		
Weird People	$5.00		
You Got to Be Crazy	$5.00		
Your Attitude Is Showing	$5.00		
SUBTOTAL			
TOTAL FROM BOOKS AND VIDEOTAPES			

Add $2.50 for shipping and handling (allow 2-4 weeks for delivery)

TOTAL AMOUNT ENCLOSED: _____

Please Print:

Name_____

Address_____

City_____ State_____

Zip_____ Home Phone_____

Daytime Phone_____

Mail to: Millicent Hunter Ministries, Inc., P.O. Box 9143,
Philadelphia, PA 19139

Please make checks payable to Millicent Hunter Ministries.

For speaking engagements, please call 610-356-8525.

Additional copies of this book and other
book titles from DESTINY IMAGE are
available at your local bookstore.

Call toll-free: 1-800-722-6774.

Send a request for a catalog to:

Destiny Image® Publishers, Inc.

P.O. Box 310
Shippensburg, PA 17257-0310

*Speaking to the Purposes of God for This
Generation and for the Generations to Come*

**For a complete list of our titles,
visit us at www.destinyimage.com**